ETERNITY, ANSWERED!

ETERNITY, ANSWERED!

REVEREND RICH MARCONI

XULON PRESS

Xulon Press
2301 Lucien Way #415
Maitland, FL 32751
407.339.4217
www.xulonpress.com

Paperback ISBN-13: 978-1-6628-6485-8
Ebook ISBN-13: 978-1-6628-6486-5

TABLE OF CONTENTS

Preface

*O*ddly, it was never my intent to write a book. What started out as rambling thoughts that I might use to reach a dear and long-time friend for Christ, eventually morphed into what you are now reading. You see, this friend of mine is one who firmly believes he has no need for God and His divine intervention in his life. Let's call him "John."

John is a man who diligently followed a career path, which led him to great success and wealth. He has a wonderful wife and son. His son has followed in his father's footsteps. "John Junior" was an Eagle Scout and has gone on to a magnificent career, surpassing his dad's success. Junior married, and he and his wife have borne three grandchildren to John and his wife.

My friend John and his spouse travel the world, explore many hobbies, and are loving life and each other. You might say they have the perfect life. Like all of us, this is certainly not true, for no one is "perfect," but he has been able to meet the hurdles of life and is appropriately proud of doing so.

When I first began witnessing to John by telling him what the Lord had done for me—delivering me from a cesspool of backsliding into immorality that nearly derailed my marriage of twenty-eight years, his answer was along the lines of, "That's good for you, Rich; I'm glad for you," never taking to heart the transformative power that had renewed my life.

My wife and I both got saved in January of 1986. As a new Christian, I zealously began bringing the news of the Gospel to my family. I got through to my Catholic mother and eventually forged a dent with my dad. One sibling, however, whom I love dearly, refused the message of Christ, for this person was deeply steeped in the New Age and progressive mindset. With that being said, my greenhorn experience with witnessing was squelched, so I chose another path: to remain silent about the things of God only to broach the subject if a door of willingness was opened to me. Never again would I "beat someone over the head" with the Bible. I placed my proverbial witness lamp "under a bushel."

In my retirement, I took it upon myself to enroll in Bible college. A branch of Life Christian University (LCU) had conveniently opened a campus at my home church in Homosassa, Florida. Among the courses I have taken thus far was a class in personal evangelism. Although I aced the class, leading a neighbor to Christ and writing a report about it, this particular neighbor had previously expressed an interest to me about me sharing God's Word with her and was a willing candidate from the start. This gave me what one might consider an unfair advantage.

I have found from writing research papers that it seems the Lord has blessed me with a knack for cogently expressing my ideas on paper, for I have time to consider all that is being downloaded into my brain without diversion and to carefully choose my words, however, not so much with thinking of my feet during a live debate. Apparently, for lack of ability to be a "street evangelist," God is showing me a new calling, writing, for the Lord God Almighty has contributed more to the pages in this book than any of the facts and figures I could glean. In fact its title, "*Eternity, Answered*," which only came after writing the final chapter, appears to have been the divine "hook" to provide intrigue to attract the curiosity of the potential reader.

Effectively, this class on evangelism had revealed to me the inadequately small amount of time I spent obeying the Great Commission by "going out and preaching the Gospel into all the world." In part, this is because many of the people I've attempted to reach are the intellectuals, the college graduates, and the everyday man who has been submerged in the world's philosophies who all have been indoctrinated into the world's supposed wisdom and knowledge.

What I've discovered since my conversion to Christ and "setting my mind on things above" is an obvious spiritual smokescreen perpetrated by, and permeating within, the halls of higher learning. What they teach, in essence, is a form of secular religion of their own making. The subject matter contained in the following pages is an effort to tear down some of these "doctrinal beliefs," some of their "sacred cows." By God's grace, it is therefore my goal to use this book as an evangelistic outreach to those multitudes of individuals whose minds have become distracted from understanding all things *truly* spiritual. This is God's way of setting me forth on the mission field of evangelism to the worldly thinker. *All glory goes to Him.* And as author and pastor Allen Jackson remarks, "Having faith doesn't mean you check your brain at the door."

Within these pages, it is my hope to draw the reader into a journey of the unknown and revelation of things unseen, into what I consider the true definition of "eternity." To the unbelievers who think mankind has all the answers to what troubles us in this world, whether that be world peace, famine, or climate change, prepare to take a tour of a different world, a higher existence. We're going to expose the unseen. We're going to "pull back the curtain."

To the believer who has run up against this same brick wall as I have, that is, the inability to make inroads with that person in your life who has been rigidly submerged in the wisdom of this world, this book may be a useful aid to reach that holdout. At the very least, my hope is to get the thinking man to think twice, at the most, to sow seed for the Kingdom of God and, at best, to save some souls. This is a mission field no different from foraging into the most remote regions of the world to bring the Gospel news to isolated peoples. Sometimes I think this modern-day intellectual mindset is just as dark and secluded from the Word of God as any isolated tribe one might reach.

To the believer who has been on the fence about going all-in for Christ, I say pick a side! Let me remind you who owns the fence—Satan.

Get off his turf and commit! Use this book as an evangelistic tool for those similar individuals in your life who stubbornly reject the Lord, thinking they know better than to believe in the "fairy tales" found in the Bible. I once was that way, too, but God changed my heart.

So I dedicate this writing, first to my beloved friend, "John," and to others like him. It is my wish that you open your collective hearts and read the full content of this book. I promise it won't take long. I thank you in advance for your readiness to be open-minded. I would also assume many of you have come into contact with some believers in Christ from within your own circle of friends. If for nothing else, when you open your mind to the things I'm about to present, you'll get a better picture of that believer's heart and the eternal One in whom they place their trust. Yet most importantly, I pray your heart, not just your mind, may be opened as well.

May God give you *His* peace, *His* understanding, and *His* wisdom. Amen.

Chapter 1

Introduction

This writing is intended for the curiosity seeker, both secular and religious. It is jointly an intellectual exercise and a spiritual quest. It is an intertwining of science and Scripture, taking what current scientific discovery has to offer against the backdrop of boundless, eternal revelation. The purpose of this book is to draw attention to the God of this universe, who created it all and has documented it in His Word, the Bible.

Man has complicated mechanisms to explain nature. God has simple answers, easy enough for anyone to understand, yet apparently too simple for the proud. To those who believe, the Scripture references I cite will most likely make sense to you. Unfortunately, biblical truths are hidden from the carnal man whose unawakened spirit and pride has blinded him to the invisible things of God. It is my hope to help remove the "spiritual cataracts" from the eyes of the unbeliever.

"Jesus is deeply offensive to the educated minds of today."[1]

So, to the humanist, agnostic, or atheist reader: I predict you will most likely ignore, reject, or scoff at these same biblical quotes that will enlighten believers. Why? The Bible has the answer to this question. "You will be ever hearing but never understanding, you will be ever seeing but never perceiving. For this people's heart has become calloused; they hardly hear with their ears, and they have closed their eyes. Otherwise they might see with their eyes, hear with their ears, understand with their hearts and turn, and I would heal* them" (Matt.13:14–15—Jesus quoting from Isa.6:9–10).[2] Therefore, for the sake of enlightenment during the course of this writing, I will intentionally bounce between some hard facts of science and the cold, hard truth of Scripture.

"The god of this age has blinded the minds of unbelievers so that they cannot see the light" (2 Cor.4:4).

You may ask, "Heal* me from what?" The answer is *spiritual blindness;* the inability to align your mind's intellect and thinking alongside your *spirit man.* We are spirit beings coursing through life in a physical body. Modernity, as if from necessity, has divorced itself from this eternal truth: that we are *spirit* first, *then* soul and flesh. So too, the modern science community embarks on its quest for knowledge at the exclusion of things spiritual. Disregarding the element that we possess within us a *spirit man* and how that impacts discovery, we are hopelessly remanded to reliance upon that which can be seen, heard, or touched using the inadequately deficient five senses we've been given. These limited senses can only perceive things within a three-dimensionally limited reality, not those things which are *unseen* and *intangible.*

Surely one may employ the use of mechanical devices that can detect those things outside our scope of perception, such as microscopic cells, colorless gases, ultraviolet and infrared light through the use of radio telescopes, electron microscopes, gas chromatographs, and mass spectrometers. But we then ignore the fact that we can't measure how we came to have understanding, feelings, and emotions. We can't measure the unexplainable and mysterious attributes which led us to this point of speculation and curiosity about eternity and our surroundings from the onset! So we dismiss this area of nature and relegate it to other fields of scientific study: psychology, psychiatry, sociology, philosophy, and the paranormal.

Missing: The Spirit Realm

It's of the gravest importance before I continue that I point out the reality of a spirit realm. Society as a whole has warped our understanding of this basic truth. I will make many references to the word *spirit* in this book. Contrary to your preconceived notions about "the devil," who has been portrayed throughout pop culture and media as the little imp taunting you on your left shoulder opposite the little angel on your right cautioning you; or the red, pointy-eared creature holding a pitchfork, wreaking havoc and all sorts of mischievous behaviors, you must know: in the unseen spirit realm, *there really are devils more commonly known as demons—and their leader is Satan.* Okay, I can see the unbelievers shrugging their shoulders! Go ahead, doubt and laugh. To me, it is proof positive of your *spiritual blindness,* which will be discussed in more detail later.

According to the Bible, these demons are fallen angels whom God cast out of heaven and dwell upon this earth, perverting the things of God and blinding the minds of men. They appear to mankind not as little red devils, but they disguise themselves as tantalizing temptations offering paths to so-called "happiness" and "contentment" without revealing the final cost of indulgence. They are the cause for all the pain, misery, and misfortune ever conceived by man. For unbelievers reading this, how they got here is irrelevant to the purpose of this writing, but the reason that demons exist may become clearer to you as you read on. The condensed version is this: the role they play as it pertains to this study of eternity has an important impact, for it explains the nature of fallen man and our free will in choosing whom to follow, God or man, the Infinite or the finite.

Implicit in the title, "*Eternity Answered,*" is this disclaimer: this writing addresses to the unbeliever what might sound implausible and impossible and can only be absorbed amidst an atmosphere of open-mindedness. Granted, I'll admit my concept of eternity is openly vulnerable and as such, subject to criticism and reproof. In a face-to-face setting, I would welcome your thoughts on the matter. What I am attempting to present here, apart from Christian apologetics, is simply an exercise in "thinking outside the box."

"For since the creation of the world God's invisible qualities—his eternal power and divine nature—have been clearly seen, being understood from what has been made, so men are without excuse" (Rom.1:18–20).

My presumptions about the eternal will be based upon biblical truths alongside current scientific observation. Nowadays, although it hasn't always been so, the science community routinely rejects God as the source of all creation, for its claim seems to be this: *As we increase discovery and accumulate more knowledge and data, the end result will be disproof of the existence of God.* I'd like to take that argument and reverse the contention. Regardless of your IQ, college degree, or level of comprehension, we are all limited in our ways of thinking about the infinite since we all possess a mere, finite brain.

A genius mathematical theorist can calculate abstract equations so complex that only a peer group of contemporaries might fully comprehend them, while the person of average intelligence naively accepts their conclusions based solely upon the belief that they're "smarter than us and know more." Over the course of time these theoretical postulations become accepted as current "fact." It will look good on paper—*until*—another mathematical equation or theory is proposed that either adds to the current theory or indicates otherwise, rendering the former hypothesis incomplete or void. In other words, theoretical science is *mutable*. It is subject to change. Case in point, around 1543, Nicholaus Copernicus theorized the orbital paths of planetary motion around the sun as being circular until Johannes Kepler came along in 1609 to suggest the orbits to be elliptical.

Apart from the classical scientific method which employs observable, tangible, repeatable, conclusive evidence, the branch of *theoretical* science remains in the realm of hypothesis, *not* fact. It is an educated guess at best. Likewise, nothing I'm positing here can be assuredly proven for lack of tangible evidence, nor can it be disproven in a laboratory with empirical certainty. As with the theoretical physicist, my observable contentions reside entirely within the realm of theory while using common sense and reasoned conjecture as my guide.

However, contrary to the secularist, I hold biblical truth *to be certainty,* for it is God who set forth all things, visible and invisible. For good reason, it is my belief He spoke into existence all laws, both *moral and intangible* as well as *physical* and *measurable* and set them into motion. His truth is *immutable;* it is *eternal truth.* His words are the same yesterday, today and forever. Psalms 119:39b–40a states: "for your laws are good. How I long for your precepts." I long for His precepts *first* as I grow more curious. I begin my quest for eternal truths from the standpoint of what Almighty God has to say about it. In the light of faith, I simply cannot reject His authority out of hand. Later, I will broach the topic of faith in God and how it is not simply "blind faith."

"He who thinks half-heartedly will not believe in God. But he who really thinks has to believe in God"–Sir Isaac Newton.[3]

This was the position of a majority of scientists long ago, namely: Sir Isaac Newton, regarding his laws of gravitation and motion and other accomplishments too numerous to list; Gregor Mendel who founded the science of genetics; George Washington Carver whose work radically changed the science of agriculture; Blaise Pascal who co-founded probability theory; Lord Kelvin who codified the first two laws of thermodynamics; Samuel Morse who invented the telegraph; Alessandro Volta who invented the first electric battery; and Robert Boyle who defined elements and compounds, invented the vacuum pump, discovered the necessity of air to fuel fire, and established his general rules for gases and the pressures they exert ("Boyle's Laws"). There were myriad others. What did they all share in common? Their starting point was, "God is world ground," meaning, in the same sense as "ground zero," scientists recognized a reverence for God and His creatorship behind every aspect of nature.

The paramount reason for my certainty which is in accordance with a biblical worldview is this: In my view, it is *because* God created us in His image (*He* being triune in nature, Father, Son, and Holy Spirit; *we* being spirit, soul, and body) we therefore bear similar characteristics. For instance, according to the Bible, God sees, we see; God hears, we hear; God speaks, we speak; God feels, we feel, God creates, we create, and so forth. Notably, embedded among these similarities we, apart from the other beasts in creation which *were not created in His image,* have this internal void: an intuitive yearning for the infinite set in place by our infinite Creator. I believe He intentionally placed this natural curiosity inside us in order to lead us to discover, not only the inner workings of nature, but *Him personally,* the eternal God who created it all.

My wife calls this our "spiritual umbilical cord" which, if not properly directed, can attach itself to destructive behaviors such as alcoholism, addictions, and such. This misalignment occurs when we, in rebellion against a moral God, deny Him as its proper connection. We are led away from the truth of God and blindly trust only in our own limited abilities. To blindly ignore this intuitive bent within us, leads the God-denying scientist to explore his trade from the wrong vantage point. Without first considering a belief in and the knowledge of God (which like other concrete data have been made available and passed down through the ages in His Word), man's only resource is the limited capacity of his own finite brain and the accumulation of data over the years. This denial of biblical knowledge was spelled out in Jesus' own words some 2,000 years ago, "For judgment I have come into this world, so that the blind will see and *those who see will become blind.*" (John 9:39).

With that being said, one cannot dismiss the importance of what has been contributed from the advancements of science. I will concede the men and women of science diligently pursue their respective fields with sincerity. They will earnestly debate the merits of their findings among themselves. Also, I will concede that the Bible leaves open much pertaining to the details of how God did what He did in the creation process. I think this was intentional. God left the door open to future curiosity seekers, scientists, to unveil the mysteries of nature. However, science's goal is empirical accumulation and formation. God's goal is spiritual molding and shaping. In the field of science, data and facts are key. In the field of theology, faith and reverence of God are of the utmost importance. I contend you must have one hand-in-hand with the other. For me, to understand eternity, one must understand the nature of the *eternal one*.

While we all have our personal concepts of eternity, infinity, and the great beyond, each and every one of these belief systems will differ based upon education, religious or irreligious upbringing, personal experiences, and countless other influences which have shaped our individual lives. Mine happens to come from a casual fascination with science viewed through the lens of a biblical perspective. Even so, our various observations and conclusions are grossly subjective, and that includes mine; for how can *any* finite brain aptly wrap itself around a dimension beyond the mere *three* dimensions through which we perceive and manifest our existence? In other words, the atheist's thoughts and conclusions, no matter how well and intelligently constructed, are equally subjective as mine, while at the same time being equally questionable!

With that being said, with the help of God's Word, let's come to explore the unexplainable, imagine the unimaginable, and seek answers to the unanswerable question: What is eternity? Where do we fit into this grand scheme? How will it be when our lives pass and we presumably become part of that eternity? After death, has our former existence here on earth been immortalized simply through a memory in a loved one's heart? Or, is this all there is and then we proceed into a great nothingness? Of course I lay no claim to holding the one key with the single answer to the infinite, nor should anyone for that matter—but please, I invite you to indulge me further.

If you are reading from a secular standpoint, tuck this thought away: isn't it true the more we delve into answers to the infinite, the more questions arise? From my standpoint, the more that is revealed, the more the nature of God becomes apparent and the more God's Word has to say about it. In the end, my hope is to arouse a fearful reverence for the all-powerful God who exists there. In actuality, *He* is the only one who truly knows for sure; hence, He is the only *true* source from whence we can derive the answers we seek. Let's get started.

Chapter 2

Eternity Large

The Infinitely Large

*I*n short, modern science is observation into the whole of God's creation. Yet at one time, mankind, like an egocentric infant wrapped within its carnal self-absorption, thought the entire cosmos, all the heavenly bodies, revolved around the earth: the sun, the moon, and the stars. This supposition conformed with the early church's conception of their relationship to God. As such, the early church in its ignorance, and because evidence to the contrary was not yet readily available, promoted this notion. But Galileo, Copernicus, and others had something to say about that. They defied the scientific norms of the time by revealing the sun as the center of the solar system—but not without resistance.

Contrary to those detractors who believe the religious leaders of that day were using the Bible to defend this untruth, it is noteworthy to mention they did no such thing. In actuality, what they were defending was the orthodoxy of the *science of that day*, which purported otherwise, and they were unwilling to face the new truths being presented that would be in direct opposition to the status quo.

So now we know the earth is merely a relatively small planet revolving around an average-sized sun (star) among hundreds of millions of other stars in our Milky Way galaxy. In fact, prior to the early twentieth century, we thought that the Milky Way was all there was to the universe. By the mid-1900s, the universe was estimated to be about 4 billion years old. But with the inventions of increasingly more powerful telescopes, among which is the Hubble Space Telescope, space has been determined at this point to contain an estimated 200 billion other galaxies, each containing hundreds of millions of stars. Now, it is currently estimated the observable universe extends out over more than 150 billion light years of space

Scientists estimate the age of the universe, marked by the "Big Bang," to be roughly 13.7 billion years old. As technology advances, as with the recently launched James Webb Space Telescope, once it completes its initial commission to study our solar system, presumably the size of the known universe will again increase and continue to bear witness to God's infinite fingerprint, His eternal nature. "The heavens declare the glory of God, the skies proclaim the work of His hands" (Ps.19:1). Yes, the infinite nature of God is revealed in His limitless creation of the heavens: "He determines the number of stars and calls them each by name" (Ps.147:4). Yet, the consensus among a seeming majority of secular physicists is that there has to be an alternative explanation. To this end, some astrophysicists have had to violate concrete rules of physics with the intent to deny giving God the credit as the reason for all we can observe.

Many years ago I watched a documentary (I think it was on the Science Channel, but no matter, it was one among dozens of similar secular nature/science shows). In the effort to explain how the Big Bang disbursed matter throughout the vastness of space in an instant, they needed a theory to justify how it occurred. A number of scientists proposed there was a moment of time where matter was scattered outward from the Big Bang event *faster than the speed of light!* Short of providing a way to achieve time travel (you know, "wormholes," "warp speed," and other such propositions) the cosmic speed limit, according to Einstein *is* the speed of light. It is the constant "C" in his famous equation $E=MC^2$ ("Energy equals **Mass** {or **Matter**} times the velocity of light {C} squared"). To exceed this speed limit would be in direct violation of one of the most fundamental rules of physics and would negate Einstein's Theory of Relativity, a stalwart of modern physics. As it is shown from this example, scientists must intentionally contradict themselves and essentially "bend over backward" to deny God as Creator.

I submit, God was there at the beginning, and He reveals to us in His Word, "God created the heavens and the earth" (Gen.1:1). Without God in the equation, it might seem to appear to the secular thinker to have been a big bang out of nothingness or some mysterious "singularity." But this too, is in fact, representative of yet another example of science "bending the rules" because this violates the "Law of Conservation" wherein it states, "Matter is neither created nor destroyed but conserved." This means it is impossible for matter to just "happen"; it can only be converted into energy, and conversely, energy can be converted into matter. The only possible solution to this event is the Creator.

The carnal man might also take exception in regard to biblical truth by asking, "How could there have been light (Gen.1:3) before God created the heavenly bodies like the sun, the moon, and the stars?" (Gen. 1:14). Here is a prime example where modern science sets out on its quest for knowledge while refusing to accept the existence of God based on a misconception of what the Bible declares. As we continue, more will be revealed about God's character and nature. In this case, it is one of God's many inherent character traits—that of *being* light. "The sun will no more be your light by day, nor will the brightness of the moon shine on you, for the LORD will be your everlasting light, and your God will be your glory." (Isa. 60:19). He was the Light created on the first day.

His nature as light is a spiritual representation that exemplifies how good overcomes evil, light representing the good and darkness representing evil. It's why we sometimes describe the overall theme of a horror flick or a tragedy as being "dark." His omnipotent character is displayed in how light dispels darkness—and not the other way around. Therefore, it could be said the "lights in the sky" created afterward are merely a portrayal of the nature of the Almighty, a clue to the common man revealing a trait of God's character exhibited through nature. Another obvious biblical picture using light to reveal God would be how sunlight is reflected from the moon: the Son of God, Jesus, being a perfect reflection of God the Father. "The Son is the radiance of God's glory and the exact representation of his being…" (Heb. 1:3a).

One can be a believer in God and His supernatural might while at the same time *not* be a science denier. It is the nature and character of God to be that of truth and order. It is in the nature of carnal man to harbor lies and sometimes create disorder. It is that carnal nature that leads men to deceive themselves and invent lies and contradictions, such as "order from chaos" as proof of a non-existent God. However, I firmly believe it is what science *continually* reveals about nature that bears out the truth of God's eternal existence and His creation, because He provided endless, magnificent, diverse evidence to extol *within that creation* His infinite glory. Though they have physical eyes to see, it is their "spiritual blindness" that prevents the unbeliever from not seeing this.

"For my thoughts are not your thoughts, neither are your ways my ways," declares the LORD. "As the heavens are higher than the earth, so are my ways higher than your ways and my thoughts than your thoughts" (Isa.55:8–9).

Infinite means, "limitless or endless in space, extent, or size: impossible to calculate." Does the unbeliever ever stop to consider why this universe cannot be measured? Is it possible this unanswerable question is posed deliberately to invoke a sense of awe and fascination of its maker? The only way this question can be interpreted is with the understanding that we, as finite creatures, must recognize our position in respect to our limitations. We are woefully inadequate to place a label on something so grand, so magnificent, and so much larger than us. Who are we to think we can? Yet wonderfully, we are dared to think this way. Why? Only one conclusion remains: we must face the truth that, in our finite thinking, we are inadequately deficient without the infinite wisdom that comes from beyond our field of understanding. We must glean from the overt clues given in what we observe to recognize there truly is a source for that sort of understanding. But first, we must overcome our self-aggrandizement while at the same time recognize we *are* significant in one regard, an importance that is also impossible to calculate: we, in comparison to "infinite smallness."

Chapter 3

Eternity Small

The Vastness of the Infinitely Small?

In light of the prevailing notion that we are but a meaningless speck in an infinite, limitless cosmos, let's now focus our attention in the other direction: to the infinitely "small." Throughout the course of science history, the concept of the smallest particle has changed. This in no way can be understood without first considering there seems to be an infinite degree to smallness as well as to vastness.

The theory for the concept of an atom was first recorded by the Greek philosophers Democritus and Leucippus in the fifth century BC. It was thought if you take a piece of matter and continually divide it, you will eventually come to a point where you could divide it no more. The Greek word *atomos*, from which the word *atom* is derived, is translated as "indivisible."

In AD 1897, the first subatomic particle, the electron, was discovered by J. J. Thomson; in 1911, Ernest Rutherford discovered the nucleus of ordinary hydrogen was a proton; and in 1932, the neutron was discovered. Since then, a branch of physics known as "quantum mechanics" was developing during the 1920s (and continues to this day) where a lengthy list of even smaller particles are being discovered. Up until this time, it had been understood there were four fundamental forces in physics: gravity, electromagnetism, the strong nuclear force, and the weak nuclear force. But the unveiling of these newly discovered subatomic particles suggested there is a fifth fundamental natural force present in the universe, yet to be discovered. This called for a new theory to unify the rapidly changing data coming to surface. To categorize these findings, a "Standard Model" was set up that included four categories of subatomic particles: (1) six different kinds of *quarks,* which basically are the make-up of protons and neutrons; (2) six different kinds of *leptons,* which are certain electrons, neutrinos, and others particles; (3) the four *gauge bosons,* which are the force carriers and the most recently discovered Higgs boson, "…an elementary particle with zero spin and mass greater than zero, predicted to exist by electroweak theory and other gauge theories, discovered in 2012. Also called: **God particle** (informal)."[4]

These particles fall into specific categories of function, some are in existence only to decay and convert into other subatomic particles within a mere 1.5 trillionths of a second. Not only do these particles exist within what was originally thought to be the "indivisible" atom, they also behave in a manner unlike the physics of the external physical world, thereby relegating them to the unique study of quantum physics. As a side note, in his effort to unite the two fields of physics, Steven Hawkings devoted a large part of his life in developing "The Theory of Everything," and wrote that "understanding the universe offers a glimpse of 'the mind of God.'" Ironically, this was from the remarkable mind of a man who sought to take God out of the equation.

According to a theory called "quantum randomness," it is suggested certain ones of these subatomic particles (bosons and fermions) can exist in two or more places at once called "superposition," making measurements of them fundamentally unpredictable. (This might be a stretch, but implicit in this thought is God showing a representation of the unseen spirit world!). Short of going deeper into quantum theory which is immeasurably above my pay-grade, the point I'm making is that there seems to always be a study leading us to understand there is *no* particle that is indivisible! Nor can any *empty* space between these particles be measured or divided.

The Size of Matter

I recall as a boy in junior high school science class, the teacher offered a crude example, a "picture" of the diameter of an atom in relation of its nucleus to its electrons. The shell of an atom was compared in width to the distance between New York and Los Angeles, with the nucleus being, say, a baseball in the middle somewhere in Kansas! The thousands of miles in between were indicative of the space within the electron shell in relation of the electrons from the nucleus.

Also given as an analogy, the nucleus of an atom was compared to being the sun at the center of our solar system with its planets, representing electrons, in orbit around the nucleus. Note: to consider this span, the time it takes light to travel from the sun to Pluto (at roughly 186,000 miles per second) is about five hours. Think about all that nothingness or "space" between the particles that compose a single atom!

Now consider this: those comparative measurements I've just stated were but *one* atom. The average human adult 180-pound male consists approximately of *7 octillion atoms!* That's written as an unimaginable 7,000,000,000,000,000,000,000,000,000 atoms! It's estimated that 5 *trillion* hydrogen atoms alone can fit on the head of a pin! Imagine now that *infinite vastness* of inner space that exists within our own bodies!

With this being said, allow me to surmise there is an infinitely vast *smallness* to complement the infinite vastness of space. So now it appears we human beings are *not* so insignificant in the grand scheme after all, not just a "by-chance" chemical formula, as some might assert. We are not a meaningless speck in all creation. In fact, considering my contention that infinity extends inward in a fashion similar to how it extends outward, this would place us human beings somewhere smack dab in the middle of all creation! The Bible puts it this way, "Do not think of yourself more highly *than you ought* . . . but rather with sober judgment . . ." (Rom.12:3; *italics* mine). The implication here is you *should* think highly of yourself for you are personally known by your Maker, the God of the universe!

As opposed to the humanist's opinion that we are insignificant compared to the grand scope of nature, an odds-defying anomaly in God's infinite, eternal economy, we are not just a meaningless speck without reason or purpose, but we are right where God has placed us, right where we belong, "for such a *time* as this," (Esther 4:14b), important to Him and His predetermined purposes for our lives. Speaking of *time*—

Chapter 4

Finite Time

Time

*W*e measure the ebb and flow of heavenly bodies to measure our years, then we subdivide the years into months, months into days, days into hours, hours into minutes, and minutes into seconds. We date time back to the prehistoric, and we extrapolate time outward into the future. That's all there is, right? Not so! Ever watch an Olympic race? Have you noticed how they've broken down seconds into tenths, hundredths, even thousandths of a second? A thousandth of a second might seem insignificant to us as it pertains to our everyday existence, but in this case it determines who gets silver and who gets gold.

Since we can't go back in time, when we think of measuring it, we usually consider time as eternally moving forward, a linear, outward left-to-right graph, that it's "large," and continues outwardly forever. However, in the science community, "inward" time is being subdivided down to the infinitesimal.

In 2020, it was reported a group of scientists at Goethe University in Germany published a study that measured the time it takes for one photon of light to cross a hydrogen molecule. Without going into the particulars on how they did it, the result was it took 247 zeptoseconds, the shortest span of time ever accurately recorded, which is this

fraction of a second in decimal form: 0.000,000,000,000,000,000,001!
A trillionth of a billionth.

But that's not all. Early twentieth-century German physicist, Max
Planck, who was better known for his contribution to quantum physics,
determined a theoretical unit of time called, you guessed it: "Planck
time." It is still considered the smallest measurement of time in physics
that has any useful meaning, and it's called a "yoctosecond." How many
Planck times are there in one second? 10^{-24}. Here's what that looks like
in fraction form to the casual observer: The number one, over a one
followed by twenty-four zeroes: 1/1,000,000,000,000,000,000,000,000—
that's one *septillionth* of a second!

Where is God?

In the Bible we're instructed to "Be still and know I'm God"
(Ps.46:10). Since God created all of this, He lives outside of time, matter,
and endless space, just as a sculptor is separate and apart from the lump
of clay he is molding. I see an implied mystery revealed in this Scripture
in that His eternal abode is found *outside* the bounds of space and
time—while concurrently being *inside* of space and time—as though
while He's apart from the clay, His hands are "soiled from the clay He's
molding into form."

He exists beyond the largest of things and within the tiniest of
particles in matter and space; outside of periods of time—a place that
cannot be measured simply because He doesn't exist within any *measurable* "time" or "space" as we know it. He is outside the yardstick as
well as inside the momentary ticking of a clock. His existence cannot be
summed up numerically. We can't put a numerical value on Him within
our physical environment. No, Psalm 46:10 proclaims that God in all
His eternal outward majesty also exists in between even the smallest,
imperceptible fraction of a second. He exists within the limitless divi-
sion of time, matter, and space, while also being completely outside all
of His massive creation!

His Signature, LARGE! (andSmall!)

At the same time, He asserts in Psalm 147:4, "He determines the number of stars and calls each by name." Eternal God, the Creator of all things, who lives outside of time and space, has stamped His infinite "trademark fingerprint" upon all that He has made to reveal His eternal, limitless nature, *larger* and *smaller* beyond all we can perceive: larger than the vastness of space yet smaller than any indivisible particle of matter; larger than the limitless possible genetic combinations yet smaller than any one-celled creature; longer than the highest number that can be counted yet shorter than a yoctosecond.

This eternal character of God can be displayed in the fact that no two falling snowflakes are identical in appearance. And to further demonstrate His eternal stamp on all creation as the original creator and designer, let me bolster this notion regarding His "fingerprint" upon all creation by saying every person (created in His image) who ever existed or will exist has fingerprints unique to him or herself; an *infinite* variety. In fact, throughout all of living nature the plethora of diverse examples bear testimony to His eternal, limitless nature!

The Alpha and the Omega

Let's get a bit more theological by introducing how God characterizes Himself in relation to time. When Moses was summoned by God at the burning bush to go and demand Pharaoh's release of His people from Egypt, Moses asked God, "Suppose I go to the Israelites . . . and they ask me, 'What is His name?' Then what shall I tell them?" God said to Moses, "I AM WHO I AM. . . . *I AM* has sent me to you." (Exod.3:13–14; *italics* mine).

The Bible calls God, (now Jesus speaking) "*I am* . . . the 'Alpha and the Omega,' the 'First and Last,' the 'Beginning and the End'" (Rev.21:13). Implicit in this statement: God is eternal. He isn't the "Was," or the "Will

Be." He just "Is." As aforementioned, He exists outside of time and space in the realm of eternity. Let's paint a picture of how this might look:

A *"Ball of Yarn"*

To draw this concept in terms we can all understand, I must use a three-dimensional illustration for God's creation. Imagine a ball of yarn floating in emptiness. The ball of yarn represents the entirety of all created matter and space, our universe, all that exists in the physical world. Outside the ball is eternity where God lives. The thread that comprises the ball of yarn is one continuous thread moving from the inside to the out, and from the outside back in, representing the passage of linear time. From God's perspective (from the perspective of eternity) the thread is rapidly in constant linear motion, the passage of time seems to randomly repeat over and over as the thread moves out and back in, a continuous loop, throughout and within the ball.

It is my belief that God, lovingly yearning for a family, created us, His children, in His image as perfect, sinless immortal physical beings, to fit into His creation that was designed in advance of our arrival to meet all our physical needs: food, water, air, and so forth (as any good father would, to provide a secure home for us). Yet because He is omniscient, seeing the "ball of yarn," knowing the beginning from the end, He knew mankind was doomed to failure and would turn their delegated authority and dominion over this earth to the devil. He foresaw His children falling into sin, hopelessly destined for the lake of fire that originally was created for Satan and the fallen angels. Despite this foreseeable outcome, the solution to save mankind lay in His Son, Jesus, who would have to shed His blood on a cross as a *substitutionary* death as the way to reach out to us to redeem us from certain death, to place us back in right standing before Him. For human imperfection, *sinfulness,* cannot coexist with godly perfection, *sinlessness.* "Even before He made the world, God loved us and chose us in Christ to be holy and without fault in His eyes" (Eph.1:4 NLT).

"*In eternity there is no past. What God is and does is all in the infinite power of an ever-present now*"⁵ With that being said, and at the exclusion of all else in creation, it is *we, mankind* that matter most to Him. So now picture that fast-moving thread, representing the passage of time along our individual life spans,from our conception to the very end of our lives and beyond, every event; every win and loss, every success and failure, every right and wrong decision. The thread, or better stated the "timeline" that is in constant motion, can be accessed by God at any given point throughout our lives, past, present, and future, in that He lives outside of the "ball," and the timeline it represents, completely outside of time. He has access to any point of time in our lives where we were damaged or traumatized, and He can touch with His finger and heal any moment of time in our past as if it were today. He can also heal us in our present moment—even the trajectory of our future because God says, "Before I formed you in the womb, I knew you . . . For I know the plans I have for you . . . plans to prosper you, not to harm you . . . to give you hope and a future." (Excerpts from Jer.chapters 1 and 29).

Yes, in the smallest degree of time, all our lives are but a vapor, a momentary flash in the pan to the one who reveals Himself in all things great and small. And all it takes for you to access His eternal glory is a single, immeasurably small moment in time.

Chapter 5

Finite Faith in Science

The "Faith" of Science: "My 'god' is King Kong"

*M*odern science contends we are very, very small in comparison to a seemingly endless universe and that the vastness of space reduces us down to a mere speck in the overall picture. This contention is further bolstered by the idea that we are here by chance and the product of natural selection, "survival of the fittest." There's the assumption that organic chemicals were somehow mystically induced through natural occurrences like primordial soup and lightning to transform organic chemicals into the breeding ground for all life. In essence, it reduces man down to a random, clever chemical compound. The chemistry of the intellectual becomes alchemy!

Charles Darwin wrote the nineteenth-century book *The Origin of Species: By Means of Natural Selection or the Preservation of Favoured Races in the Struggle For Life."* Interesting, what has "race" got to do with it? But I digress. In the book, he asserted the future fossil record should uncover *multitudes* of connections between species. In over 150 years, no such transformative connections between species have yet been uncovered. In fact, a number of so-called "missing links" were found to have been hoaxes, for example, "Piltdown Man" and "Nebraska Man." The remainder of so-called "links" are speculated to be "humanlike remains." In particular, the remains of Nebraska Man (actually only one tooth, a molar), was touted as the "missing link" used in the Scopes "Monkey Trial." Years after the trial was settled, which subsequently launched Darwin's theory into the public schools, it was found this tooth turned out to be that of a pig. Was there a retraction from among scientific circles? Not much. Was this news splashed across the headlines in major news outlets? Nope. Did the secular public schools renounce the study of evolution? Of course not! Now, thanks to an imaginative artist's conception, we're given the chart of the ascent of modern man walking left to right from monkeys to gorillas into men. This "picture" is systematically inculcated into our collective psyche and infused into the minds of our young.

Darwin also conceded that if scientific study progresses to a point where it finds evidence to the contrary, *his theory should be thrown out.* In Darwin's own words, he stated this in his book:

> I am well aware that scarcely a single point is discussed in this volume on which facts cannot be adduced, often apparently leading to conclusions directly opposite to those at which I have arrived. A fair result can be obtained only by fully stating and balancing the facts and arguments on both sides of each question, and this cannot possibly be done here. . . . If it could be demonstrated that any complex organism existed, which could not possibly been formed by numerous, successive, slight modifications, *my theory would absolutely break down.*" (*Italics* mine)

Sadly, nowadays when a person of faith refutes his theory, his objections are shouted down with contentious accusations of being ignorant, a "flat-earther," or worse. However, if I should dare to become guilty of the same mean-spiritedness, the same could be said for the secularist. I contend, today's acceptance of evolution is a similar absurdity to the popularity of the eighteenth-century concept of "Spontaneous

Generation," a concept that lingered from the time of Aristotle who originally proposed it through the middle ages into the 1800s. This widely held idea persisted despite evidence to the contrary that arose. In 1668, Francesco Redi conducted an experiment that dispelled the belief that "maggots arose spontaneously in rotting meat.."[6] Scientific observation to the contrary was also introduced in the mid 1600's by microscopist, Antonie van Leeuwenhoek whose work contributed to the studies of bacteriology and protozoology.[7]. Ultimately, the argument for Spontaneous Generation was fully *disproven* by Louis Pasteur in the nineteenth century and finally put to rest.

However, despite the illogic of today's evolutionists' stubborn acceptance of the presumption that life sprang up spontaneously some unimaginable eons ago, Darwin's theory now flies in the face of knowledge that has surfaced regarding one-celled organisms. These one-celled creatures at one time were considered "simple" life forms but now have been shown to possess complicated mechanical and chemical complexes within and without. Among the complexities of single-celled organisms are the ability to move toward food via flagellum (hair-like "paddles"), feed upon other organisms and liquid matter, and replicate itself via asexual reproduction. An amoeba, when confronted with unfavorable conditions, forms a protective covering around itself called a cyst. This cyst contains a substance called "chitin" that helps it to reproduce.[8]

Amino acids function as the building blocks of proteins which are essential to catalyzing the vast majority of chemical reactions within a living cell. Mid-twentieth-century biophysicist, Pierre Lecomte du Noüy put it this way. He affirmed that "the chance formulation of a typical (*simple*) protein molecule consisting of 2,000 atoms is in the order of one to the 2.02×10^{321} or practically nil" (statistically impossible). He went on to say, "Even if the elements are shaken up at the speed of the vibration of light it would take 10^{243} *billions of years* to get the protein molecule for life."[9] (*italics*, mine). Also cited from Ramm's book is a quote from L.J. Henderson, an early twentieth century biochemist, where he states in reference to factors necessary in nature to make life possible: "the world is comparable with a single throw of the dice. And common sense is not foolish in suspecting the dice to have been loaded."[10] Apparently this brand of common sense is not so common today.

What also is not considered in the evolutionary process is the Cambrian explosion. This was a period of time, supposedly 500 million years ago, where there seemed to be a "big bang" of diverse life forms bursting on the scene worldwide. It appears from the fossil record, this all occurred rapidly; it was an "all-of-a-sudden" appearance of practically every major animal phyla. In other words, it is proof-positive that so-called "intermediate organisms" on the lengthy evolutionary scale appeared *simultaneously*.

Mid-twentieth-century physicist Sir James Hopwood Jeans, who is credited with playing a major role in the development of quantum theory, pointed to how all of nature is analogous to mathematics, that all scientific knowledge is mathematical in form. Essentially, modern-day theoretical physicists present their calculations from observing the cosmos in mathematical equations, for example, $E=MC^2$. Jeans proposed the assertion "the universe being mathematically described and mathematical in form is on the order of pure thought."[11] Therefore, the belief in *order out of chaos* is absurd because everything in nature is ordered. Examples of this would be the periodic chart of elements, the order of seasons, and the unmistakable perfect storm of organic life in symbiosis with an extensive inorganic recipe of elements and substances in nature, which support life. And it is a *fact* that "chance and time" eventually lead, not to order, but to rot and decay.

When closely examined, Darwin's theory lacks logic or any real proof. There has been no conclusive experiment which ever produced "life" in a laboratory from organic substances. Nor has there otherwise been any empirical evidence to confirm his theory to be a fact, yet as *fact*, this theory is currently being presented in virtually every branch of secular education. Fossil records are unclear, and still no "missing link" between species has turned up while fossilized human footprints *have* been discovered alongside dinosaur footprints! ("Paluxy Man"). Yet, this fact is rarely reported if not outright ignored and belittled. Wikipedia dispels the validity of the finding by claiming them to be "elongated dinosaur tracks" and dismisses it as a hoax, but the pictures clearly show they are footprints of human origin.

"Old Earth vs. Young Earth"

Carbon dating and other similar radioactive methods of dating fossils are based solely upon assumption and conjecture from the prevailing worldview of secular scientists. Carbon 14 is an unstable carbon atom with a half-life of 5,730. This means the radiation being emitted reduces by 50 percent every 5,730 years (the loss of its additional two neutrons, forming stable carbon 12). They take the subject item, say a fossil or a bone, and measure the amount of carbon 14 it contains relative to the amount of stable carbon 12. But first, it can only be randomly *assumed* what quantity of carbon 14 the specimen originally contained. Additionally, they then establish this ratio as a constant, relative to the assumed amount of atmospheric carbon 12 and its isotope carbon 14 with the *presumption* the atmosphere was at "equilibrium" during the time the sample existed. It is entirely conjecture based upon the prevailing narrative of an earth believed to be billions of years old.

However, these estimations do not take into account the biblical report of a diluvian flood, evidenced partly by marine fossils upon high mountains. A catastrophic upheaval caused by a worldwide flood would have had a monumental effect on atmospheric carbon. This is because the oceans regularly absorb and emit carbon according to the earth's natural cycles of heating and cooling in the forms of carbon dioxide and its many other chemical combinations. When closely examined and you take away the assumptions, the results of carbon dating and other similar radiometric dating methods (e.g., Uranium 238 decaying down to lead) can vary from a few thousand to millions of years! Again, in order to make the theory fit the narrative, the scientist must first start with assumptions that never take into account a biblical flood and reject the Word of God out of hand. "Let God be true and every man a liar" (Rom.3:4).

Over the years within evangelical circles, there have been numerous opinions regarding the age of the earth, whether it was a local or world-wide flood and many other unanswerable questions. Theological theories abound that contend various viewpoints on anthropological and geological questions. One such school of thought is "Moderate Concordism," where it is believed when God created everything, it was made to look as though it had been there for some time, meaning Adam was created as a grown man, say thirty years old, the trees had rings that might indicate hundreds of years of growth, gorges and mountains were set in place appearing to be ancient, and the heavenly bodies appearing to be billions of years old.

And there's "Progressive Creationism," which substitutes for the word *day* in the creation account to mean eons, (taking 1 Peter 3:8 out of context, "that one day is as a thousand years with the Lord, and a thousand years as one day."). It purports God brought about His creation over the course of millions, if not billions of years, which conforms to the geological and astronomical records. Yet, in either case, it is God doing the creating.

But when all debate is set aside, there are certain tenets we hold that align us all together in the faith. That is the belief in the intersection of time and eternity that occurred when Jesus came on the scene: Christ crucified for the forgiveness of our sins at the appointed time—Period. Whether God created the earth in six twenty-four hour intervals (of which I am a supporter) or countless eons does not impact the fact that this universe was miraculously brought into existence by the mere breath from God's lips.

Music as Another Clue to Eternity

In the realm of God's spiritual kingdom, the number seven has great significance. It is the number of "completeness." "By the seventh day God had finished the work He had been doing; so on the seventh day He rested from all His work" (Gen.2:2).

Fittingly, the number eight has eternal implications. The reason for this is what comes after the here-and-now—that which was completed on the seventh day—the eighth day. In a manner of speaking, eternity, the infinite is represented by what comes after the finite—the "eighth day of creation."

In his yearly devotional, *The Book of Mysteries*, Jonathan Cahn, a Messianic rabbi, talks about this particular topic, "The Mystery of the Eighth Day,"[12] In short, Cahn refers to the Hebrew Festival of Tabernacles that lasts for seven days. The day after this feast in Hebrew is called "Shemini Atzeret," which translates to, "the gathering of the eighth day." It essentially implies the "day after the end of days," the day when God gathers His believers unto Himself.

In the book of Revelation, the final book of the Bible which deals with end-time prophecy, there are numerous images of sevens: seven churches, seven angels, seven lamp stands, the seventh seal, the seven bowls of wrath. Toward the end of the book, after all creation is renewed and redeemed, you find no mention of the number seven again. The time that follows finite time has arrived, and the infinite has come—Eternity, the eighth day.

While considering this theme, have you ever wondered how music came to be? That is, what is music's importance as it pertains to the eternal? In the previous paragraphs, we talked about the seven days of creation. Having been an amateur musician for most of my life, I have come to understand some basic principles of music theory, chord structure, and so on. What's most interesting about the standard musical scale is there are seven distinct notes to every scale, regardless of sharps and flats or whether they are major or minor scales.

We've all come to regard this concept in the simple song, "Do-Re-Mi" from *The Sound of Music.* You know, "Dō (*doe*) a deer, a female deer, Re (*ray*) a drop of golden sun . . ." It is the child-like example denoting a standard major scale. If you count out, *do-re-mi-fa-sol-la-ti-do* you come to the number eight. That is because the eighth "dō" note is the "octave" above the original "dō" note. They are the same note only an octave apart. On a piano, the scale of C is the simplest to see and understand this. When it's played, the notes go **C-D-E-F-G-A-B-C**, all on the white keys.

The standard upright grand piano has, curiously, (!) 88keys on its keyboard, so if you start from left to right, from the low C in the bass register to the higher notes, one can play seven octaves of the scale of C. But notice how every time you repeatedly reach the next C note, the "eighth" note, it automatically becomes the "one" note all over again for the next progression of the scale.

Now imagine a piano keyboard extending out forever in each direction, with an infinite amount of octaves, that number eight repeatedly continues to become the one again, and again, and again—the first day of creation over and over! Hidden away on this imaginary keyboard is yet another glimpse of eternity that God gives to the one whose eyes have been spiritually opened. Pictured in this marvelous example: His eternal kingdom is constantly being renewed, forever being created! It is an awesome spectacle if we attempt to stretch our imaginations in that direction.

Science has its place in the unraveling of answers to nature's mysteries and its eternal principles, but it can lay no claim to the Christian's brand of faith. All of what modern science believes is based solely upon the minds of men whose limited capacities and sinful tendencies are to color the truth. Mortal man will never know the end from the beginning, for his source material is not founded upon the eternal will of an eternal God. No physical answer forthcoming will ever encompass the entire scope of what is essentially endless, for every finding will open yet another door to the infinite. As I stated at the beginning, there is no mind on earth intelligent enough to grasp this concept of eternity, *nor ought there be.* For only God is the keeper of this knowledge. Graciously, to the believer by divine revelation, God reveals snippets of those things we need to know, when we need to know them and whenever our humble and contrite hearts are open and ready to receive them.

Chapter 6

Eternal Faith in God

The Complexity of Life

Inherent to all current scientific assumptions and theories, at best, they can only theorize and hypothesize, stretching the opinion to fit an overall narrative. Or they claim that, "science has not *yet* discovered this, but in time . . ." At worst, one might argue (yes, *I* might argue!) that it takes more faith to believe complex organisms came about purely by chance without the aid of an almighty Engineer directing its design.

Ironically, the same brand of resistance the early church spewed against emerging science discoveries coming forth during the Middle Ages exists today, only this time, conversely, the science community against the body of believers. This occurs even in the face of when modern science uncovers facts that align with the biblical perspective. Case in point: the complexity of DNA structure, the basis for all life. The Bible states, "I am fearfully and wonderfully made" (Ps.139:14). The DNA molecule is in essence "computer coding" of the highest degree, far beyond anything created by man. Despite this high degree of engineering, Christians who defend *intelligent design* are defined as "flat-earthers" and "science-deniers" by those hostile to the biblical worldview—and with disparaging virulence.

Yet an inescapable fact is this question: How long did it take for the Human Genome Project to computer-sequence the human DNA molecule with the aid of super-computers? *Fifteen years.* And what exactly is DNA? It is the magnificent blueprint for all life forms, mechanical drawings in the highest degree of detail, and harder still to understand how it came to be.

It is virtually impossible to fully understand how genes along the helix of a DNA molecule can carry biological information, let alone transmit that info via messenger RNA to inform each and every cell in a given organism what to build. This applies also to any particular life form it instructs and the accompanying organs and mechanisms thereof. It determines whether it becomes insect or plant life, animal or human, fish or fowl. Further, it assigns its corresponding body parts, its eyes, hair color, organs, every system upon system all interdependent one upon the other. It enables the organism itself to become animated! I could go on, but I think you get the picture. It is a most complex "computer coding" beyond anything ever conceived, miles above the comparatively miniscule playing field of Bill Gates and Steve Jobs.

I will not attempt to cite one particular study in statistics, for there are numerous such studies to support both the religious and secular viewpoints. The usual variable to support "chance" creation is a bias toward lengthy time periods. But with logic and common sense, one must conclude without any doubt, it is statistically impossible for random atoms and molecules to independently form themselves into what appears to be a highly deliberate and intelligent pattern. Here's a clever quote from biologist Edwin Conklin: "The probability of life originating by accident is comparable to the probability of an unabridged dictionary resulting from an explosion in a printing shop."[13]

Statistically and yes, realistically impossible, there are not enough eons of time for all this to have fallen into place "by chance." Take just the human eye, for example. How does an eyeball, through an evolutionary process, *independently* develop a lens, a retina, optic nerves, and myriad other counter-components having no similarity one to the other, come together all by themselves to create an organ that will provide, by electrical impulse, vision to the brain that is yet another organ? How did the various molecules in the eye "know" these processes needed to take place in order to form *itself*? How did blood vessels "know" to provide the eye with capillaries to provide the proper nourishment and oxygen to support the cells' functions? The complexity of just this one example is astounding. But there are thousands of examples of various sight organs in other living organisms that allegedly "evolved" *differently* across the spectrum of countless other species; alligators with translucent eyelids, hawks with keenly precise, far-sighted vision, raccoons and other nocturnal animals with night vision.

This enigma is characterized by the expression, "Irreducible Complexity," which argues it is impossible for a given organ (or, "biological system") within a complex organism to have evolved in successive, small modifications independently from the pre-existing functional system/mechanism to which it corresponds. In simpler terms, how did the optic nerve "know" to form itself to connect the eye to the brain? Evolution teaches lower forms evolved into higher forms incrementally in small, successive modifications. This assertion fails miserably in light of the obvious truth that organic matter does not inherently possess knowledge and skill to perform what would otherwise appear as miraculous.

I would submit, it takes a measure of faith *far* greater than the most fundamental believer in God as the Designer and Creator, to believe this all happened by chance. Another question: Is not statistics considered a mathematical science? Ironically, in the case of evolution, this science is manipulated by the use of inventing *improbable* variables. When the statistics show probability unfavorable to their argument for evolution, they invent increasingly longer periods of time in order to fit the likelihood of that "one chance in a gazillion" to promote the theory. Granted, this could go on ad nauseam because as more is revealed about this expansive universe, its seemingly ever-increasing size and age, the more ammunition they'll gain.

Dr. Neil T. Anderson, who worked with NASA on the Apollo space program in the 1960s, has touched on this when he quoted this in regard to building the space shuttle: "The technology to build the type of rocket it would take to boost that size payload into space had not yet been developed, but NASA believed that given enough time and resources, it could be done. Ten years later it was. *Some who believe only in science exhibit greater faith than Christians.* How much more should we be able to accomplish if the object of our faith is God?" (*italics, mine*) [14]

Yet, due to a "faith" in science over faith in God, modern science willfully denies that we are "fearfully and wonderfully made" by an omnipotent designer and dismisses the impossible odds borne out mathematically in order to further their beliefs.

"I think, therefore I am" - René Descartes.

This secular "faith" seems also to ignore the begging question regarding the intangibles of life, how we *philosophically* "evolved" into self-awareness and curiosity and how we came to have a concept of moral behavior. And who decides what is moral and immoral, what is "bad" and what is "good?'And why are there unsettled thoughts within us all that beg the questions: "Why am I here? When will I die? Where will I then go?" And the most pressing question of all, as this writing asserts, "Where does the universe end? What is forever? What is infinity? Where does eternity end; does it end?"

We can all agree that among the various life forms on the earth, sadly it is only we humans who know our days are numbered and have this inherent, intense curiosity, a void we feel compelled to fill. All other living beasts and creatures have natural instincts but don't possess the innate sense of the eternal. Only mankind—*because we are created in God's image, His Eternal image*—has this instinctual, inborn sense of the eternal. I would suggest it's a void only an eternal God can fill because He has placed it there to begin with to lead us by way of inborn curiosity to discover Him! But the natural, fallen man has no concept of the things of God. Ecclesiastes 3:11 states, "He has also set eternity in the hearts of men; yet they cannot fathom what God has done from beginning to end." Only the spiritually *reborn* person can begin to understand this.

A Faith That Works—God's Path

In accordance with the tenets of my faith, whenever a person gets "saved," his or her spirit, once dead, is now made alive and reunited with the living, Holy Spirit of God and becomes a saint of God. At the time of conversion, the newborn believer has chosen to give his or her life over to the will and care of the heavenly Father's Son, Jesus. Now, because the two spirits are newly joined, this makes the person "one with Christ," an adopted son or daughter of the living God.

Before being converted, God in His sinless perfection, could not have fellowship with us for we had the imperfection of sin. But God the Father now sees Christ—His perfect likeness—living *within us.* We were once sinners destined to hell, but by the blood offering of Jesus, our sin has been *paid* for, covered and removed. "For the *wages* of sin is death, but the gift of God is eternal life in Christ Jesus our Lord" (Rom.6:23). Our formerly dead spirit has been resuscitated and restored to immortal perfection. But because we still occupy these physical bodies that were born into sin, the end result, death, remains for our "outer shell." For the Bible declares, "The wages of sin is death."Yet, because we are now identified with Jesus' substitutionary death and resurrection, we too will be resurrected to a new, immortal body. "But Christ has indeed been raised from the dead, the first fruits of those who have fallen asleep [meaning, "died"]. For since death [sin] came through a man [Adam] the resurrection of the dead also comes through a man [sinless Jesus]. For as in Adam all die, so in Christ all will be made alive" (1 Cor.15:20–22).

At the moment of conversion, God goes to work in the saint's life, healing deep-rooted traumas from the past, His "finger" literally touching the *"timeline,"* healing those moments in the believer's past where he was afflicted physically, mentally, and spiritually. The believer is healed as if the incarnate Jesus crossed the span of time into today ministering as He did some 2,000 years before, touching and healing throngs of followers. God has access to that "thread," the "ball of yarn," in cooperation with the surrender of the new believer whose mind is being transformed and renewed into the image of His Son. This miracle of transformation occurs internally in the presence of the Almighty, all-knowing God of all eternity, working His healing process through time and eternity.

About God's Triune Nature

I need to pause here to examine the triune nature of God because in the last couple of paragraphs I have delved into the salvation work of the Godhead being the work of three distinct personalities, Father, Son and Holy Spirit. Some folks use the three physical properties of water to describe the Trinity, that is, liquid, ice, and steam. Each are water, H_2O, chemically, the same substance. But this example does not fully cover it. Simple math shows a better example.

Yes, God is one. And Yes, God is three in one. How can this be? In finite terms, one could dispel this argument by simply saying, "one plus one plus one equals three." But our God does not only add to us blessings, He multiplies! So to bring my point to bear, I can alternately say, "One *times* One *times* One equals One." Or, one ∞ ("*infinity*") times one ∞, times one ∞, equals one ∞. Admittedly, this may seem like a quaint assertion to you, that is, my use of finite mathematical standards to define an infinite quantity. However, since infinity has no subdivision, it cannot be added to, or subtracted from.

The Bible clearly portrays a triune, creative God of all eternity using parables as examples. Jesus spoke about the seed that fell upon good soil in the parable of the sower. "Still other seed fell on good soil, where it produced a crop—a hundred, sixty or thirty times what was sown" (Matt.13:8). In this parable, Jesus was describing the effect of the Word of God (the seed) upon the man (in his fertile heart) who "has (spiritual) ears to hear," that His Word, sown into the heart, would have a multiplying effect in his life. There are also the accounts of Jesus feeding the five-thousand (Matt.14:13–21) and also, four thousand in another passage (Matt.15:29–39). What did Jesus do with the five loaves of bread and the two fish? He *multiplied* them!

His Triune Nature Personified

The most essential aspect of God's character is *He is Love*. He not only loves, the meaning of the word *love* in this sentence being a verb; but God *is* Love, a proper noun in this case (1 John 4:8). With this in mind, how is it that an eternal being who has always existed since eternity past be "Love?" Doesn't love need an object of its affection for it to abound? Does not love extend out to something beyond ourselves? Unless one is a narcissist, love can only be true and real and perfected once it is shone upon the object of its affection. So to whom did God extend His love? God the Father loves God the Son who loves God the Holy Spirit! And you can rearraange that sentence backward and forward because within the Godhead, there is perfect Love flowing between the three Persons of the Godhead.

This truth is revealed in the very first chapter of Genesis:"Then God said, 'Let *us* make man in *our* image, in *our* likeness, and let *them* rule over all the earth' . . . So God created man in His own image, in the image of God He created him, male and female He created *them*" (Gen.1:26–27, *italics* mine). As you can see, male and female were considered as "one being," as depicted in the marriage covenant, "the two will become one flesh." When both are united to the Spirit of the Living God, they become *triune* in nature. Man and woman *together* were originally considered one "Adam." It was not until *after* the fall of man that Adam, now spiritually separated by sin from his wife and from God's Holy Spirit, he named her "Eve."

Let me end here with this. The picture painted by God in His ordination of the marriage covenant with Adam and Eve, "The two will become one flesh," is an exact replica of the Godhead. It is impossible to separate the three personalities within the Godhead, all of them being one. Surely you're familiar with the statement given in most wedding vows, "What God has joined together let no man put asunder." Marriage is a picture of eternal God's covenant with finite man. It is even derived from Scripture that the (worldwide) church of believers are, "the bride of Christ." Jesus is the bridegroom who is coming some day for His bride, a very intimate portrayal of a loving relationship between God and mankind.

In this fallen world behind the spiritual curtain is the sinful puppet master, Satan, perverting the marriage covenant in the minds of men. The ideal of a natural man/woman marriage covenant, God's design that brings forth life as a result, (it "multiplies" humanity), has been re-defined and altered to destroy God's picture of His perfect love for us. This highlights how sinful mankind will resort to any measure to reject God's will for their lives in pursuit of their own self-gratification. It is clear evidence of man's innate rebellion against God and His purposes in orderly nature. Similarly, it is how science rejects the very notion that God is evident and supreme in all of nature. "For this reason God sends them a powerful delusion so that they will believe the lie and so that all will be condemned who have not believed the truth but have delighted in wickedness"(2 Thess.2:11–12).

The delusion mentioned herein is the worldwide spiritual blindness that dominates all cultures. It permeates throughout all of academia, media, and everyday social exchange. Yes, if you are unwilling to believe or you are one who has rejected out-of-hand God's truth found in His Word, you are among the lost souls who have been scammed into believing the physical world is all there is. It is a lie from author of lies himself, Satan.

But there's hope. You need not continue to live a lie. You truly are among the offspring of a heavenly Father who loves you. You were created in His image to be an image-bearer of our eternal Father. You have merely strayed away from knowing Him and have either never known or forgotten the true purpose for your existence. Believe this: the Lord, Father God is eagerly expecting to hear from you. He offers *free salvation* through His Son, our Lord Jesus Christ. As pictured in the story of the Prodigal Son, (Luke 15:11-32), He wishes to have you back and welcome you with open arms! He wants to shower you with His love, mercy, grace, and protection. The eternal God of the universe loves you enough to die for you—*and He did*—to save *you* from believing the lies that lead to eternal damnation.

Chapter 7

The Great I Am

"It's Not Blind Faith"

Throughout the Old Testament are found extensive genealogies and prophecies regarding the lineage and the coming of our Lord Jesus Christ, which were foretold hundreds of years before. Some Bible scholars contend there are over 300 Scriptures pointing to Israel's Messiah. What's foretold about Him describes His place of birth, His bloodline (through King David and others), His tribal affiliation, Judas' betrayal, His crucifixion, and so forth. Using only *eight* of those prophecies that are historically proven facts about Him from sources other than the Bible, the probability of only eight being fulfilled would be one in 10^{17}. In the book *Science Speaks*,[15] Peter Stoner and Robert Newman discuss the statistical improbability of one man fulfilling the eight. Here's the scenario they paint:

> "Suppose we take 10^{17} silver dollars and lay them on the entire face of Texas. They will cover all the state two feet deep. Now mark one of these silver dollars and stir the whole mass thoroughly, all over the state. Blindfold a man and tell him that he can travel as far as he wishes, but he must pick up one silver dollar and say that this is the right one." Imagine now the statistical improbability

of *300* prophecies being fulfilled in the one person. One might say, it's "infinite."

Here is what the Bible says regarding the incarnate Jesus who went about His ministry healing and enlightening the masses. According to Scripture, time and eternity had an appointed moment to intersect. "But when the set time had fully come, God sent His Son, born of a woman, born under the law to redeem those under the law, that we might receive our adoption as sons" (Gal.4:4). What occurred was this: through Jesus, Eternal God became fused together with carnal man (the infinite with the finite), "For in Christ all the fullness of the Deity lives in bodily form" (Col.2:9).

Born of a virgin and impregnated by the Holy Spirit of God, Jesus' bloodline, severed from the bloodline of Adam, was devoid of the sinful nature of man, more specifically, the "seed of Adam." No sinful nature was passed on to Him, that which is passed on to all of us sinners, the descendants of Adam. Jesus was born *fully God* (the seed of the Holy Spirit of God) and *fully man* (born of the flesh of a woman).

So while time as we know it was moving steadily "left to right" across a *horizontal* graph of the past into the present on into future, Eternal God in the form of the incarnate man Jesus, *vertically* intersected time with eternity at the precise moment, "For I came *down* from Heaven . . ." (John 6:38a).

In Jesus' Own Words

Jesus himself offered some veiled descriptions to what I am referring. Addressing the Pharisees, He asked, "What do you think about the Christ? Whose son is he?" They answered, "The son of David." Listen closely to Jesus' reply. "How is it then that David, *speaking in the Spirit*, calls him 'Lord'? For he says, 'The Lord said to my Lord: Sit at my right hand until I put your enemies under your feet.' If then David calls him 'Lord,' how can he be his son?" (Matt.22:42–44, *italics* mine). Dissecting this statement, we see David being quoted from Psalm 110 (one thousand years prior) speaking "*in the Spirit*" as if from David's vantage point, *at that very moment,* he could prophetically see the coming Messiah, *his Lord,* while at the same time realizing Him (Jesus) to be his own descendant. David speaks *in the Spirit realm* of one instance separated by one millennium. "With the Lord a day is like a thousand years and a thousand years are like a day" (2 Pet.3:8).

Moses witnessed the burning bush from which came the voice of God. God was instructing Moses to become the agent of the Israelite's release from bondage in Egypt. In his insecurity, Moses said to God, "Suppose I go to the Israelites and say to them, 'The God of your fathers has sent me to you,' and they ask me, 'What is his name?' Then what shall I tell them?" God said to Moses, "I AM WHO I AM. This is what you are to say to the Israelites: 'I AM has sent me to you" (Exod.3:13–14). Clearly, God has stated herein His eternal nature. He has no beginning and has no end. He just *is.*

From this example comes Jesus speaking again to the Pharisees and said, "Your father Abraham rejoiced at the thought of seeing my day; he saw it and was glad." In response, the Jews responded sarcastically, "You are not yet fifty years old and you have seen Abraham!" Listen to how Jesus answered, "I tell you the truth, before Abraham *was* born, *I am!*" (John 8:56–58, *italics* mine). Not only was this a clear proclamation of His divinity, but also a crystal clear picture to how God lives outside of time and came in the flesh to demonstrate His presence among us. To signify the intersection of the eternal with the finite, He verbally intermixed the past tense with the present tense. Additionally, He paints a picture of how Abraham, the father of our faith, prophetically (just like David, *in the Spirit*) saw Jesus in a moment of time in the future, while living out his life in faith as if it had already actually occurred, roughly 2,000 years prior.

As it is with the incredibly remote odds of prophecy coming to bear, finding that "one silver dollar," it is not with blind faith that we believers place our trust and lives in Jesus. What Jesus spoke here on earth two thousand years ago is what His Father spoke thousands of years before. Biblical prophecy also emphasizes Jesus' future return for His church. As surely as the unforeseen came to pass in predicting Jesus' arrival on earth, most assuredly, too, will His return be. The truth of God's Word was validated in Jesus. God's character never changes. His truth is rock solid. His laws, physical and moral, are impeccably fashioned. When we open our spiritual hearts to His truth, we too see ourselves living in the light of eternity witnessing His presence as if He were here today, standing before us, just as He did when He revealed Himself to Abraham and David. This eternal truth can be yours as well.

Chapter 8

Eternal Salvation

Everlasting Forgiveness

Psalm 103:12 reads, "As far as the east is from the west, so far has He removed our transgressions from us." The overarching point that arises from this passage of Scripture is the infinite quality of His forgiveness. Had He said, "As far as the north is from the south," there would be a finite end. For as we travel northward, we come to the North Pole. By continuing in the same direction of travel, we now find ourselves moving southward. But if we travel east, and continue to travel east, we will continually, *forever,* encircle the globe, never changing direction; likewise traveling westward.

Isaiah 38:17B reads, "You have put all my sins behind your back." Implied here is a God who forgets my sin! So how does an all-knowing, almighty God remove our sins as if they never occurred and "forget"? Let's step back to our topic of time and its infinitesimal nature.

Remember, all of creation is reflective of the eternal nature of God, the designer. Whereby time can be reduced down to incredibly small segments, juxtaposed against the concept of an incredibly long span of time infinite in length, we must again recall how our Creator exists outside of time and space. Time has no bearing on an eternal God; He has no beginning or end. Time itself is as much a part of His creation as is material substance. Therefore, according to Second Corinthians

5:17, "If anyone is *in Christ,* he is a new creation; the old has gone the new has come." It goes on to say in verse 19, "God was reconciling the world to Himself *in Christ,* not counting men's sins against them" (*italics mine*). Notice I emphasized "*in Christ*" twice. The reason for this (at least for me!) is mind-blowing. Verse 21 reads, "God made Him who had no sin to be sin for us, so that *in Him* we might become the righteousness of God."

My point is this: God lives outside of time and space. Christ is God in the flesh. Jesus' arrival in time and space intersected time at the perfect moment in order that all prophecy would be fulfilled in His appearance on earth. When we are *in Christ,* we take on in our spirit a new nature, the indwelling of the Holy Spirit. The moment this occurs, *that moment in time,* marks the advent of our eternal life. The consequences of our sins are cast aside, thrown into the depths of the sea. For all intents and purposes, our spiritual lives in the time prior to our arrival in eternity had never existed! God's eternal presence aligned in my spirit creates in me His eternal nature.

"For the message of the cross is foolishness to those who are perishing, but to us who are being saved it is the power of God" (1 Cor.1:18).

Speaking personally of my own salvation, it was the "Adamic nature" (my sinful nature) that was nailed to the cross. I, being identified "*in Him,*" the human Jesus was there taking my punishment. He took my place. It was there *I* died to sin 2,000 years ago. And when the glorified Jesus was raised from the dead, so too was I identified, "in Him," as risen from the dead. I have become a new creation *in Christ.* "The old has gone, the new has come" (2 Cor.5:17). I have been reborn, "born again," "born from above." I am now spiritually re-created in the image of His Son, Jesus. Because He loves me, He exchanged His righteousness for my unrighteousness. There He paid the penalty for my sin. In the grand scope of eternity, I believe the moment I accepted Christ into my heart was exactly the same moment Jesus declared, "It is finished" (John 19:30).

When God looks at those who have invited Jesus in, he does not see the sinner; he sees the saint; not what we once were, but who we now have become in the *new* "bloodline," not of Adam, but now of Christ. We are now being transformed from within through the transfusion of *His* blood and the renewing of our minds from our old ways of thinking. He now sees the potential in what He originally saw in us; what He described as "our purpose." "'For I know the plans I have for you,' declares the Lord, 'plans to prosper you and not to harm you, to give you hope and a future'" (Jer.29:11). He sees in us "the new man," Jesus, not "the old man," Adam, because we are "*in Him.*"

"If we claim to be without sin, we deceive ourselves…" (Jam 1:8a).

You may ask, "But even those who have accepted God's plan of salvation continue to sin—what happens then?" I take you back once again to that "yoctosecond" of time. Our past sins have been removed. The moment we sin again, in a flash, that very moment becomes "the past." Overall, we submit to His will. We turn from our sin and have confidence in the God of truth, that His Word is final. Although we falter, our sins have been forgotten, past, present *and* future! For what is "the future" but yet another moment that will instantly vanish into the past, making it too, obsolete. We walk in the light of truth knowing we are not condemned and therefore aspire to live as God would have us live. We choose to not sin and are helped through the power of the Holy Spirit not to sin. The born-again believer is not sinless, he merely *sins less.*

It is only by the gift of the Holy Spirit that our spiritual eyes can be opened and come to the realization and conviction of our sinfulness. I don't expect the carnal man to understand this. "The person without the Spirit does not accept the things that come from the Spirit of God but considers them foolishness, and cannot understand them because they are discerned only through the Spirit" (1 Cor.2:14).

Most, if not all, prior to being saved by grace think they're "good people." But they live according to a code outside of God's ways. Even I used to think it was allowable for me to steal from a big corporation because their resources are inexhaustible and they have insurance coverage and tax write-offs to ease the blow of their losses, a "Robin Hood" philosophy of sorts. But I would *never* steal from a friend!

At that time I subscribed to the wisdom of this world which was my sole influence. Like a constant barrage of propaganda, I would hear the musical refrain, "You—who are on the road—must have a code—that you can live by."[16] Sadly, there was no mention of God's eternal wisdom in that sentiment. So I invented my own code that seemed suitable to me. Had I been caught stealing back then, under man's law, I would surely have had to pay the penalty of my crime for living outside of man's statutes. Consider, too, the child predator or the serial murderer; by what code is he led? So, who gets to decide right and wrong?

When we disregard *God's* moral laws, we place ourselves under the curse of His law. When we live outside His will for our lives in behaviors contrary to His perfect will by an act of our own willfulness, we situate ourselves apart from His protection. It's as though we ignore mom's warning to look both ways before crossing the street. We step out into the unknown at great risk. We therefore *voluntarily* put ourselves under a curse because of our refusal to obey what God has set forth for us—*for our own good,* His good and perfect will. We place ourselves in jeopardy when we disregard the lifeline, Jesus, whom God offers to us. And because of spiritual blindness we discount the notion of God and proceed headlong into the darkness totally unaware, defiantly oblivious. In other words, we bring upon ourselves the curses that God warns us about. It is not God who curses us; it is our unwillingness to obey His cautions against the resulting consequences of our actions.

But because of God's grace, He reached down from His infinite abode into the finite realm to provide forgiveness through His incarnate

Son. Despite knowing the wondrous beginning from the disastrous end, Almighty God, the maker of all things, *still* created us out of love for a family of children, knowing full well He would have to subject His only begotten Son (*Himself!*) to a torturous punishment to save those children from an eternal death!

It is *this* that humbles me enough to *want* to please my heavenly Father. I wish to do His will; I am eternally grateful for His sacrifice. I am pleased to live a life worthy of His grace and die to the lies of the promises of this world. It is an internal example of how I would feel outwardly indebted to someone who rescued me from a burning building. I would say, "I owe my life," to that person. Jesus gave His life in an effort to save me and fallen humanity. He died for you. He died for me. I owe Him my life. I must now die to my sinful self—*for my own good!*

Here's a remarkable quote from A.W. Tozer for you to consider. It sums up the life of the believer:

> "In every Christian's heart there is a cross and a throne, and the Christian is on the throne till he puts himself on the cross. If he refuses the cross he remains on the throne. Perhaps this is at the bottom of the backsliding and worldliness among Gospel believers today. We want to be saved but we insist that Christ do all the dying. No cross for us, no dethronement, no dying. We remain king within the little kingdom of Mansoul and wear our tinsel crown with all the pride of Caesar, but we doom ourselves to shadows and weakness and spiritual sterility."[17]

Chapter 9

God's Laws versus Man's Laws

God's Laws

God, the Master Builder, set forth all natural laws, all of which science has been grappling with throughout history. Galileo, Newton, and Einstein have carefully observed planetary motion, gravity, and physics. These laws were set in place to provide order and stability. Any random fluctuation to any of the four known physical forces, gravity, electromagnetism, the weak nuclear force, and the strong nuclear force, would propel the entire cosmos into chaos. Every outstanding scientific achievement ever made were tributes to the perfection of the grand design and nature of our maker. "Out of chaos, order?" Not without a perfect design from a perfect God, Mr. Nietzsche. It is my belief that mankind's ability and curiosity to put answers to these questions was designed specifically by God to lead us to the knowledge of Himself.

If we are expected to believe that our existence came from some random roll of the dice, how then can it be explained although we exist within a tangible, physical world, we possess intangibles, such as thoughts, feelings, emotions, and a sense of right and wrong? And who decides what is right and what is wrong if there were no purpose to our very being?

Left to man, we've clearly seen evidence throughout history of the failure to achieve societal perfection. The "peace and love" hippies of the

'60s, most of whom subscribed to a theory that boasts we are descended from apes, proclaimed, "Do you own thing," and "If it feels good, do it." It was as though, because we are by nature animals, it's okay to act like one. The result of this "worldly wisdom" produced a path to infidelity in marriages, fatherless households, promiscuity, and debauchery. Ironically, the hippies' symbol, the peace sign, oddly resembles a stick-figure of Jesus on the cross, "The Prince of Peace," turned on its head (See "pyramids" depicted in chapter 11).

The Result of Man's Laws

God created Eden, a utopian world perfectly suitable for mankind. It remained perfect until Adam and Eve messed things up and introduced sin and death into the equation. Since then, imperfect mankind has been unsuccessfully attempting to regain that perfection in the world at the refusal of accepting God's perfect plan. The utopian ideals found in Marx and Engels's *Communist Manifesto* heralded "equality of the masses," which thus produced socialism/communism, as adopted by Russia, China, Cuba, and others. This wayward thinking, apart from God's ways, resulted in the deaths of 100 million souls in the twentieth century alone. And this number excludes the extermination of over six million Jews in Hitler's Nazi Germany. Yet, in all its failure, people today are led by their own code of "good intentions" who mistakenly believe in man's "basic goodness." Ignoring man's sinful nature, they seem to want to repeat this tragedy all over again.

Defying God's physical law of gravity by leaping from a tall building, believing you can fly, will surely lead to your physical death. It is the same with God's moral laws. God is perfection. "God is not a man that He should lie" (Num.23:19). He is Truth, He is Goodness, He is Perfect, He is Love. That is the condensed version of the character of God. He has more positive attributes in His character than there are grains of sand on all the seashores on earth. Therefore, God's physical *and* moral laws are perfect. Like attempting to defy His law of gravity, breaking His perfect moral laws *also* lead to death. Certainly not immediate phys-ical death initially, but that invariably comes to us all. Violating God's moral laws results in, and maintains in us, *spiritual* death. The sad fact is, we are born that way, born to oppose God's moral laws. The clearest example of this comes out of the expression, "You don't have to teach a child how to be bad."

We are born body, soul, and spirit. The body, obviously, is our flesh. Our soul is our mind, our thoughts and emotions, our will, and our personalities. It's what secular psychology calls the id, the ego, and the superego. It is what makes you, you. Missing from this psychological explanation is the spirit, our spiritual nature. At birth, it is *stillborn*. It is born *dead to the things of God*. That is the part of us that was originally perfectly connected to our eternal Father before the fall of man, when "Adam walked with God in the cool of the day."

In brief, God initially gave authority and dominion over the earth and all its bounty to Adam—with God, his Father, as the sole authority. There was a perfect spiritual connection between Adam the son, and God the Father. Adam was created for immortality. Adam was given one job: to oversee the garden. Adam had only *one* rule to obey: not to eat from the Tree of the Knowledge of Good and Evil. When Adam disobeyed God by eating from the forbidden tree, he severed the perfect connection he had to God, breaking the chain of authority under which Adam was subject to the Father. By trickery, the serpent (Satan) deceived both Eve and Adam, causing them to disobey God. By their free will, they listened to and obeyed the devil. Thus the authority originally granted to them over the earth was usurped, and by default, the devil instead was handed authority over the earth and became Adam's master.

Our ancestry, our *seed*, extends back to the garden from the seed of Adam and Eve. They forfeited their authority and dominion of the earth over to Satan. This resulted in a severing of our "living" spirit to the Father and His authority. Mankind's spirit was now severed from the God of life and reconnected to death which came from being under the authority of Satan, "the thief who comes to steal, kill, and destroy,"

(John 10:10). By believing the devil's deception, "You will *not* certainly die," and obeying his lie, our spirits, originally connected to *life* in and through God, the giver of life, we were rendered dead under the control of Satan through whom comes death, both spiritually and physically. The removal of the God-breathed life force from within our spirits resulting in a disconnection from God's Spirit, rendered us *spiritually* dead, now with a mortal body that would soon decay, bringing *physical* death to us all.

Afterward, when approached by God, Adam and Eve, now spiritually disconnected from their Father, had become ashamed to discover themselves naked. Their nakedness was both actual and symbolic of the fact they no longer lived "covered" by the protection of a loving Father. In a desperate attempt to undo the deadly mistake, they dared to "cover their own sin" through their own works by sewing together fig leaves. This demonstrated an attempt to undo the offense by trying to cover their own sin and shame in their own strength. They attempted to reconnect to God by their own power. But unfortunately it was too late. Sin and death had already been unleashed by them into this world and served only to separate them from the Father. Sin (imperfection) is incompatible with sinlessness (perfection). Imperfect mankind could not undo the flaw and restore the perfection God had ordained. And because God cannot go back on His Word, (He is truth), God Himself could not take back the authority He originally assigned to and entrusted with Adam. Figuratively, Adam could not put the genie back in the bottle, for he had by free will reassigned his authority over to Satan.

But God Himself, in His *first act of mercy*, covered their nakedness and their sin with the skins of an animal. This was a portrayal of the first blood sacrifice needed to cover sin that led later on to the slaughter of countless oxen, bulls, goats, lambs, sheep, and birds for sins committed under the Mosaic Law (the Ten Commandments) given on Mount Sinai. This was also a sign of things to come: there would be no forgiveness for sin without the shedding of blood.

Presently under the New Covenant, it is only through accepting *Jesus'* blood sacrifice, the work of the *perfect sinless man,* that mankind can be redeemed from the very curse he brought upon himself. Jesus, as a man, had to die for man's sin, for it is written, "But you must not eat from the *tree* of the knowledge of good and evil, for when you eat from it you will certainly die." So the Father sent His Son, Jesus to die as a curse *on a tree* to redeem us from the curse we inherited from our carnal father Adam, when he and Eve ate from the forbidden tree.

How the World Dismisses God's Plan

Born in the natural, Adam's bloodline runs through us all, and so does his rebellion against God under the authority of Satan who instigated this rebellion in the first place. With Satan at the helm, he rules over all the earth and all its unsaved inhabitants propagating lies into the minds of mankind who are haplessly blinded and duped. Every idea, thought, and concept of this world's "wisdom" distracts and leads us all astray from the truth of God. All things—from man being descended from apes to the "big bang" that occurred out of nothingness to every false religion of the world—are perversions of the supernatural power and truth of God who created all things.

Instead, we place our delinquent trust in the possibility of UFOs, higher intelligences from other worlds, and science fiction. Some look to psychics, channels, Ouija boards, palm readers, horoscopes, and tarot cards for answers to supernatural questions. All these are products of the carnal mind, while ironically for the same reason many people in the world deem these spiritual things too, as illusions and sleight of hand.

Many in western cultures have convinced themselves there can be no reason or possibility for the supernatural, let alone the eternal state of the Godhead. Hence, unsaved folks consider Bible stories fairy tales. "For the message of the cross is foolishness to those who are perishing, but to us who are being saved it is the power of God. For it is written,

'I will destroy the wisdom of the wise; the intelligence of the intelligent I will frustrate'" (1 Cor. 1:18–19).

But a supernatural God He is. It is well documented among the annals of secular historians that Jesus walked the earth. Those closest to Him bore witness to His miracles, death, and resurrection. Some of His closest disciples wrote what they had witnessed firsthand: Jesus rebuking the raging storm, walking on the water, multiplying the loaves and fishes; His miraculous healings, lepers being restored to wholeness, the blind receiving sight, the deaf and mute healed, the lame jumping for joy, and people resurrected from the dead. Jesus predicted He would be put to death and rise on the third day, fulfilling scores of Scriptures written hundreds of years before. Some five hundred people saw Jesus after He was raised from the dead—all eyewitness accounts. It is not through blind faith that we who believe come to our belief and trust in Jesus. Yet it is with blind faith in theories about "singularities" and "evolution" that today's scientists place their trust.

Today's detractors, especially in the field of science, desperately wish to discredit this miraculous intersection of time and eternity, man and God. They discount the Gospel account of convinced followers bearing witness to the truth of Jesus' life of supernatural events, even unto *their deaths*. But they readily accept mutable theories, assumptions, and inferences for facts. No one was around at the time of creation, yet they earnestly think they know better than what Eternal God, *who was there,* says in His Word! It is to my regret how some of these elite thinkers place more importance in unproven theories, thinking they're right, rather than having an open mind to the invisible things that can't be explained away with science. They find wonderment in the mysteries of nature's creation but haughtily believe that in their brilliance, they can uncover all the answers, all the while ignoring the realistic likelihood of a Creator who is the one who enabled them in the first place to think in the abstract!

If only they'd place as much value in God's absolute moral laws as they do in His absolute physical laws! But ironically, they foolishly endeavor to muster up enough faith to believe in far-flung theories they can't prove or accurately assess. Their measure of faith seems to exceed that of the average believer in Christ who takes the Word of God to heart—except for sound reason.

To stubbornly ignore the obvious eternal signature of this grand creation is to place oneself in a seriously dangerous position. This peril comes to you compliments of Satan's delusion that imbeds in your "rational mind" the idea that *he* does not exist, that there are no devils and there is no God. "A fool says in his heart, 'There is no God.' They are corrupt" (Ps.14:1). Carnal man is spiritually blind to the darkness of his own heart. "The heart is deceitful above all things and beyond cure. Who can understand it?" (Jer.17:9).

Chapter 10

The Religion of Science

Science: A Modern-Day Religion

"Follow the science!" That's today's mantra for numerous reasons, most of which exist to demonize religious beliefs. Because the world is ruled by Satan, the father of lies and deception, unbelievers hold this motto in high regard. So much so, that when the argument is turned in the opposite direction, those same people will stubbornly profess falsehoods as facts. Case in point is gender dysphoria. The science says if you have an XX chromosome, you're a female. If it's XY, you're a male. And our observable physical anatomy bears out this obvious truth. And this is so throughout the animal kingdom. Not so with some of today's "elite thinkers." Philosopher Rene Descartes was quoted as saying, "I think, therefore I am." Nowadays, this dictum has mutated into a boy saying, "I think I am a girl; therefore, I am a girl." With no science (or common sense) to support it, doctors today will accommodate this warped thinking with transgender hormonal therapy and surgery. Yet the evidence shows a transgendered male still has inherent male muscle mass over and above that of a female athlete and subsequently will outperform the finest of natural-born women athletes. (Who are the *science deniers?*). The absurdity of this confusion is spelled out best by Oswald Chambers when he states, "Sin (inherently inside of man) has made the foundation of our thinking unpredictable, uncontrollable and irrational."[18] -*My Utmost For His Highest*, June 23.

Oh, No! We're All Gonna Die!

Take the subject of climate change. Over the centuries, the earth has undergone numerous climate variations from cool to warm and back. The most significant reason for this is the warming and cooling of the sun, which occurs cyclically, over which we have no control whatsoever. But the doomsday prophets ignore this fact. All of sudden, they say carbon is the culprit that is causing damage to the world, and mankind needs to step in to prevent apocalyptic calamity. It seems the "climate hysteria gang" fails to note the science behind the balance in nature.

Every creature, warm and cold-blooded, takes in oxygen and expels carbon dioxide (CO_2). In the case of humans, we exhale CO_2. Every form of plant life *takes in* CO_2 and *emits* oxygen; a beautifully designed symbiosis. The more CO_2 introduced into the atmosphere, the more and the healthier our plant life; hence, more life-giving oxygen and the more edible vegetation and more sustenance for all. This fact completely dispels the warnings of over-population, famine, and starvation.

The percentage of CO_2 in our earth's atmosphere is a mere 0.03% or, *three hundredths* of one percent. Even with the addition of so-called modern-day carbon-emitting sources like the internal combustion engine, this level steadfastly maintains this meager amount. I would submit the alleged "greenhouse" effect would be a mathematical impossibility. The output of the 1991 eruption of Mount Pinatubo in the Philippines alone emitted more carbon dioxide and toxic sulfur dioxide into the atmosphere than of all the mechanical fossil-fuel machines since the beginning of the industrial revolution. And that was but one eruption among thousands. Has anyone heard reported a dramatic spike in the earth's temperature, or any coastal city engulfed by a rising sea level? Of course not! This example is but one proving man's earthly wisdom being influenced and corrupted by the author of lies himself, Satan.

"You are of your father the devil" (John 8:44).

Have any of the apocalyptic predictions of the past come true? The answer is an emphatic *no*. In the early '70s, an impending ice-age was all the rage. In the '90s, it was "global warming." When the meteorological data failed to support that prediction, the narrative was altered to "climate change." This way, no matter which direction the data fall, they're covered. Any disruption to a normal weather pattern becomes suspect.

Back in 2006 Al Gore released his book, *An Inconvenient Truth*,[19] in which he predicted a rise in CO_2 would melt the polar ice caps, causing the oceans to rise over the next twenty years with coastal cities like Miami being submerged. At the time of this writing, sixteen years hence, there has been no measurable rise in sea levels. Greg Wrightstone, a geologist who has written a rebuttal to Gore's book called *Inconvenient Facts*, in a live presentation (https://youtu.be/59bHCuJuJw) offered this simple test: place ice cubes in a glass of water. Note the water level. Now allow the ice cubes to melt down until all that is left in the glass is liquid water. Now look at the water level and compare. The water level stays the same.

From my own knowledge of the properties of water, when water is frozen into its solid state of matter, the ice expands. The northern ice cap virtually floats upon and displaces the water, causing it to rise. This can be compared to entering a tub full of water, and as you lower yourself down, the water level rises. The northern ice cap is floating upon water causing the overall water level to be raised. If the polar ice cap were to completely melt down into the liquid state of the water, it would naturally contract. Whatever water is "added" to the sea from the melted ice would be cancelled out by the lack of water displacement; in other words, no noticeable difference in sea level.

Wrightstone goes on to note there have been warming and cooling trends throughout earth's history caused by natural forces. He also uncovers a glaring omission from the climate alarmists. The main greenhouse gas is not CO_2, but water vapor! Most media sites show a pie-chart of greenhouse gases showing CO_2 at 63 percent, methane 19 percent, and "other" as 18 percent. The true percentages of greenhouse gases are water vapor 90 percent, CO_2 6 percent and "others" totaling 4 percent.

Wrightstone also reveals several naturally occurring warming and cooling cycles in recent millennia. The warming trend that is now upon us has been continuing since 1695, coming out from the "Little Ice Age." And sadly, cooling trends during periods lacking atmospheric CO_2 caused freezing and less vegetation, resulting in starvation. In fact, we remain at a critically *low* measure of atmospheric CO_2 at the present time compared to periods of warming in the recent past, as when Greenland was actually "green" according to the Vikings and citrus fruit grew as far north as Hadrian's Wall in England during the early Roman Empire!

(Note: At the time of editing, Wrightstone's post cited above had been removed from YouTube. For more information on his work, visit: https://inconvenientfacts.xyz/. This fact is very telling. It proves my point how the world shuts down any discussion contrary to the carnal narrative being presented).

Yet, the spiritually blind are being led by the spiritually blind and continue to perpetuate the narrative of their false assertions. Those who challenge the status quo are characterized as heretics. And naturally, tax dollars don't flow in the direction of any study where there is found dissent against the norm. This is characterized more recently with Alexandria Ocasio Cortez's "Green New Deal," which could put in place useless, drastic taxation measures and coercive energy policies, directing huge sums of money to the lapdog industries who support the phony effort to stem the rise of CO_2.

Case in point, during the Obama administration, over $500 million in loan guarantees were doled out to Solyndra, a California-based solar panel company that went bankrupt due to cost overruns. It was later revealed a quid-pro-quo of hundreds of thousands in donations funneled from Solyndra executives to the Obama campaign in exchange for the loans.[20] "For the love of money is the root of all kinds of evil" (1 Tim.6:10).

This and so many other ruses being perpetrated by Satan and his minions have corrupted the collective minds of the intelligentsia. This is because mankind has been led to believe he is the master of his own destiny and in full control over everything, including the arrogance to think one could control the earth's climate. Behind every notion of man without the guidance, leadership, and protection from an all-knowing, all-powerful, eternal God is that they are being controlled, lured and conned by the evil one. The Bible clearly states, "Our struggle is not against flesh and blood, but against the rulers . . . authorities . . . powers of this dark world and against spiritual forces of evil in the heavenly realms" (Eph.6:12). Little does spiritually blind humanity realize or detect the puppet master behind the curtain, like the phony wizard in *The Wizard of Oz*. The true believer cannot buy into this ruse. It is deception, the main tool of the devil. "We know we are of God, and the whole world lies in the power of the evil one" (1 John 5:19).

This is part and parcel of my contention that modern science has devolved into a false religion of its own. It has a unique doctrine based, not upon divine revelation, but on the limited, finite boundaries of the observable things of nature. Its dogma is staunchly set against the invisible things of God, thus making man into a god unto himself. It is essentially what the Bible calls idolatry: worship of the creation, not the *Creator*.

It is interesting at this point to note how the vast array of unbelievers in higher education, including some secular scientists in the world target the God of the Bible as the culprit for all the world's ills. It is suggested that God and religion are responsible for all wars, and therefore, the world would be better off without them; that instead of following God, we should "follow the science."

When a person swears, is it the in the name of Buddha? Is it in the name of Mohammed? Is it in the name of Allah? Is it in the name of Krishna? No. In virtually every case the name of the Lord being taken in vain is "Jesus" or "God." This to me clearly depicts how the world hates the God of the Bible, and I firmly believe the reason for this is man's stubborn desire to covetously hold onto his carnal nature. It is direct rebellion against God. But God opposes the proud, those who unwittingly enjoy their lives of sinfulness.

The God of the Bible taught the Israelites not to worship anything in creation, but the one and only true Creator of everything, "YHWH" (Yahweh) or "Jehovah God." Unlike the pagan nations surrounding Israel, the Israelites were directed by God not to worship the sun, the moon, or the stars, or inanimate objects made of metal, stone, or wood. There were to be no superstitions about nature, nor any barbaric practices, like offering children to these foreign "gods." God clearly ordered nature to serve as the clockwork around planting and harvesting, about which many of their holy festivals were observed. All of nature served for grounded, rational purposes for the Israelites. The Israelites were also forbidden from consulting mediums and spiritists. They were to confine their worship and praise to Almighty God who provided them with all their needs.

Not so with the religions of the other nations. It was sorcery, astrology and false spiritism that dominated those cultures. The Babylonian, the Assyrian, the Greek, and the Roman cultures all fell into this category with a plethora of gods and superstitions; pantheism. The entire world was devoid of belief in the one, true God. Most current religions of the world fall into this grouping *in this day and age* in one form or another.

Virtually every world religion apart from the Judeo–Christian worldview direct their worship toward something *in nature* and apart from God. They create God in *their* image, not the other way around. They suppose God to be something He's not.

You'll find within this line of thinking a wide range of belief systems. This is true with the belief systems of eastern cultures that hold sacred certain animals and believe in reincarnation (Hinduism), or the belief one can attain some form of enlightenment or achieve "Nirvana" by performing more good deeds to outweigh the bad, (Buddhism) or, that I can "save myself," making man himself (the creation of God) a god unto himself. The major religions of the world fall into this pattern. They have rules and laws and dictates to follow in order to please God and earn the right into paradise. This is the "works" mentality; *man reaching up to God.*

An extreme example within this spectrum would be how the devil counterfeits the Catholic ritual in its Satanic worship depicted in a "black mass." Satan worship might involve debauchery and the spilling of or drinking the blood of an animal or worse, another human being, blaspheming the blood sacrifice of Jesus. In this case, too, man has taken the work of God into his own hands, creating a "god in his own image" in the effort to nullify God's intent of having created man in *His* image.

Christianity, by default, falls under the category of a "world religion." But it is *not.* It is the *only* belief system where God *reaches down to man.* God has provided the means by which man can attain righteousness. God accomplished this through His Son, Jesus, who did the work of righteousness for us by taking away our sin upon the cross. God's mercy is not contingent upon the works of a fallen man. All a believer has to do is simply accept *by faith* the free gift: the work that the *perfect man* has done *for* us who are imperfect. It is through a *relation* with His Son we are saved. "For it is by grace you have been saved, through faith— and this is not from yourselves, it is the gift from God—*not by works,* so no one can boast" (Eph.2:8–9,*italics* mine). As such, in this regard, Christianity is not a religion *about* God; it is a relationship *with* God.

The reason Christ died for us? It is because Father God wants to reestablish the family connection to His creation of mankind and share eternity with each and every one of us who believe. Only a perfect (sinless) being can relate to God face-to-face. God recognized from the outset that man, as a fallen, finite creature could not attain this level of perfection and that any attempt to do so would fall short of God's standard of moral, infinite perfection. The Father recognizes the work on the cross that Jesus accomplished, shedding His blood as the once-for-all sacrifice for the sins of all of humanity. Belief in His Son is the *only* requirement necessary for salvation and the *only* way to heaven. Being *in Christ*, taking *His* righteousness upon us, is the only way fallen man can attain that level of infinite perfection needed to relate to the Father face-to-face.

As much as this may sound narrow-minded to the unbeliever, this is not exclusive but *available to everyone.* "With your blood you purchased men for God from every tribe and language and people and nation" (Rev.5:9b). "Enter through the narrow gate" (Jesus speaking; Matt.7:13a). If you accuse God of being narrow-minded about becoming *spiritually* "born-again," you must also accuse Him of being narrow-minded about being *physically* born. There is only one way to enter into physical life: a sperm must be sown to fertilize an egg to become a living organism. In the Spirit realm, it is the same; a *seed* (the Word of God) must be *sown* upon the *fertile heart* of a believer for him to come *alive* in Christ. It is the only way to come into the presence of the living God.

"For broad is the road that leads to destruction, and many enter through it. But small is the gate and narrow the road that leads to life, and only a few find it" (Jesus speaking; Matt.7:13b–14). Yes, the Bible predicts this narrow path, but it is only because God knows the beginning from the end, how too few will see and accept the way in preference to holding onto their sinful lifestyles. Please, don't become a statistic!

We Must Save the World! Our Path to Nirvana!

Now, we come to how this all relates to the "religion of science." A religion is characterized by these three main distinctions: attitudes, beliefs, and practices. Take the examples of false science listed above. In each case, you'll find clearly spelled-out tenets of "faith." In the case of gender, this is an *attitude* based entirely upon "feelings" where one must stretch their logic and rationale to accept *by faith* (not empirical evidence) a tenet, or *belief* that purports to claim a person can identify as the opposite sex (which happens to be an abominable practice according to God), despite the obvious contradiction.

In the case of climate change, don't the doomsday predictions of impending meteorological disasters show a similar parallel to the *practice* of Old Testament prophecy? The prophet Jeremiah predicted the coming destruction of Jerusalem and the seventy-year Babylonian exile. " This whole country will become a desolate wasteland, and these nations will serve the king of Babylon seventy years." (Jer. 25:11). The difference from one practice being a false religion and the other being true is the prophecy from God *came to pass*. The Israelites returned to rebuild Jerusalem after seventy years of exile. "The land enjoyed its sabbath rests; all the time of its desolation it rested, until the seventy years were completed in fulfillment of the word of the LORD spoken by Jeremiah." (Jer.36:21).

The doomsday scenarios framed by the climate gang have not. The scare tactics of secular man almost always tend to prove false. Regrettably, valid Bible truth gets rejected by secular man as a fairy tale, while the false results from the predictions of carnal man conveniently get forgotten. Blindness in their false belief system remains. They arrogantly prefer to believe the lie.

A vast majority of people in this world are disinterested in the eternal things God. The eternal truth of God is ignored while the transient, elusive things of this world are coveted with the utmost importance. Satan has blinded the minds of unbelievers to the extent that they accept every passing fancy, regardless of how contradictory, outrageous, or irrational. This is because they've elevated themselves to deity status, placing their trust entirely in carnal man whose entire existence resides in the temporal. Their only attachment to things eternal are the computations, theories, and assumptions of the zealous "priests" of higher learning who fervently inculcate into the minds of the masses their own brand of religion that ignores the eternal source of true, heavenly wisdom.

Chapter 11

The Religion of God, a Roadmap to Eternity

A Roadmap to Understanding Ourselves and Our Place in Eternity

*W*ithout a sober reckoning of the eternal, without a better understanding of the ways of God, we will be forever paddling our feet in the hamster cage to no avail. We can attempt to explain all of creation with science, but science has shown itself to be untrustworthy in the hands of sinful men. The only reliable source is the God of the Bible. God gives us the essentials to right living and truthfulness providing an honest starting point from whence science can proceed (Genesis). It's an eternal, spiritual book authored by God's Holy Spirit over 1,600 years through forty spiritual men being led by the eternal Holy Spirit of the living God. It is to man what a car's owner's manual is to the vehicle.

You may think we believers simply read the Bible, but the Bible reads us. It can stop you cold in your tracks as it reveals aberrant behavior, and it can set you free from the lifelong baggage that encumbers you, keeping you blindfolded from truth. It will give you insight into things eternal and give clarity to things in this world that are unclear. It explains the myriad of mankind's misguided behavior you see all around you and throughout history.

But mainly, it guides you into the eternal principles of life: faith, hope, and love. These are the most important of all things pertaining to our lives, the greatest of which is love. While science devises its own brand of faith, one of conjecture, theory, and man's inferior wisdom, the *superior* wisdom of the God of Bible presents a full picture explaining the hows and whys of imperfect human behavior in comparison to the over-arching perfection of His wisdom as portrayed by the natural world.

God is immutable. He always was, always is, always will be. He is the "Great I Am." He lives outside of time and space. His Word remains for all eternity. The event of creation coming into being is the same to Him as this present moment. Have you considered that farthest empty void in space 150 billion light years away? He is there right now. God is omnipresent. Because He is eternal, He is as much there as He is here—150 billion years ago and right now in the present, all in the same instant! He exists in the very moment of creation *and* right now in the present moment *simultaneously*. And not only in this moment, but He also exists forward in time. He speaks of a future heaven and earth to come, for He is as much there as He is here today. Again, I emphasize, speaking in the eternal sense, there is no "time" where He comes from, for where He exists is only one continual moment, smaller than that yoctosecond! Oswald Chambers puts it this way, "The baptism (*or indwelling presence*) of the Holy Spirit does not make you think of time and eternity—it is one amazing, glorious *now*."[21]

"The Lord said to Job: 'Will the one who contends with the Almighty correct Him?'" (Job 40:1).

There was once a Broadway play (perhaps still running somewhere) based on the Gospel of Matthew entitled, "Your Arm's Too Short to Box with God." If you're an unbeliever, thinking you know better than to believe in "fairy tales," can you honestly say you know for sure? Do you think if there is a God, He's no match for you, that you know better how to run your own life? At the close of your life, I promise this will occur—you will be made aware: "'As surely as I live,' says the Lord, 'every knee will bow before me; every tongue will acknowledge God'" (Rom.14:11). When you find yourself standing in eternity before Him, do you think you will outwit Him? Do you think your case will hold water?

Let me ask you a few questions. Are you infinite or are you finite? Clearly the answer is finite. Next question: How can you be sure what the infinite will look like, especially using your finite thinking? (Let me answer that one, you *cannot*). Third question: Can you not see that you are programmed into the world's way of thinking? By that I mean don't you just accept things you don't understand simply because you got it from someone much smarter than you? And don't you sometimes find yourself mindlessly humming a jingle or thinking of an expression that has been engrained into your psyche? If you can answer any of these questions without any trepidation or doubt of what I'm suggesting, that you have become programmed by the world's way of thinking, well good for you. But think again.

Unless you've been enlightened by the truth in the Bible, all, *yes, all* of what you've been spoon-fed by the secular world in regard to God *have been lies,* or at the very least, they've been distortions. "We know we are of God, and the whole world lies in the power of the evil one" (1 John 5:19). You are party to a world of lies. In the court of law, a lie, or perjury, is a punishable felony. It's the law. In God's courtroom, a lie is also a punishable offense, but no different from murder!

Revelation 22:15 reveals this frightening point, painting the grim picture of those not saved by grace standing outside heaven's gate: "Outside are the dogs, those who practice magic arts, the sexually immoral, the murderers, the idolaters, and everyone who *loves and practices falsehood.*" Yes, liars are lumped in together with murderers. In God's economy, sin is sin. *Period. All* sin comes up short of perfection. And the kingdom of this world perpetuates this pitiful condition.

"I will destroy the wisdom of the wise; the intelligence of the intelligent I will frustrate."(1 Cor.1:19).

There are *only two* distinct spiritual kingdoms in the world: God's eternal kingdom and Satan's temporal kingdom. God's kingdom is the flipside to all of what you see around you in the physical world. It is opposite to what carnal man holds as valuable. God's ways are counter-intuitive to our basic carnal nature. Using an analogy for anyone who has ever tried to master the game of golf, it is like the hacker starting out for the first time without taking lessons. He grips the golf club like a baseball bat and swings as hard as he can to "send the ball over the fence." But what happens is he sees the ball trickle off the tee box or driven aimlessly out of control. But with instructions from a professional, we're taught to grip the club *awkwardly* and *swing easy* to allow the weight of the club head to propel the ball farther. It all seems counterintuitive at first, but once we develop the skill, we see the difference, and our game improves. So it is in God's kingdom. We *humble ourselves,* allowing *God's power* to work through us.

Here's a brief list contrasting the world's spiritual systems, Satan's earthly kingdom, versus God's heavenly kingdom:

The World Says:	*God Says:*
"Well, nobody's perfect!"	"All have sinned and fallen short of the glory of God"
"What is truth?" (Pontius Pilate)	Jesus: "I have come to testify to the truth"
"Government will eradicate poverty"	Jesus: "The poor you will always have with you"
"If my good works outweigh the bad, I'll get to heaven" (many roads to heaven)	Jesus: "*I* am the way, the truth and the life; *no one* comes to the Father but by *me*"
"Imagine there's no heaven, no hell below us"[22]	All mankind will face judgment, some to life, others to death

76

"Don't get mad, get even."	"Vengeance is mine, says the Lord"
♪ "You, who are on the road, must have a code that you can live by."[23]	"Keep *my* commands and it will go well with you."
"Seeing is believing"	Jesus: "Blessed are those who have *not* seen and yet have believed."
"Believe in yourself"	Jesus: "Believe in the Father, believe also in me"
"Go for the gusto" (selfishness)	Jesus: "It is more blessed to give than to receive"(selflessness)
Desire the lifestyle of the rich and famous	Jesus: "Truly I say ... this poor widow has put more into the treasury (two small copper coins) than all the others." (Luke 21:3)
♪ "It's my life and I'll do what I want."[24]	Jesus: "Whoever loses his life for me will find it"
"The message of the cross is foolishness" (to those who are perishing)	"but to us who are being saved it is the power of God."(1 Cor.1:18)

These two kingdoms are polar opposites of the other. The citizens of Satan's kingdom are the spiritually dead; *this includes each and every one of us as duped subjects prior to being saved.* Again, we are *all physically* born into this sorry state of perpetual death. Your body, mind, and unborn spirit are all destined to die, *eternally.* The citizens of God's kingdom are the *spiritually* revived, the "born from above," or so-called "born-again" believers in Christ. They are those who have allowed God's *living* Spirit into their hearts to resurrect or awaken their dead spirit to things eternal. A man's natural *inborn* spirit is aligned with Satan and causes eternal death and darkness. A man's *newborn* spirit is being made alive *in Christ* and has life everlasting. Simply stated, Satan= death; Christ = life.

▲ . . . . *The Poor Masses at the Bottom*

I'll paint another word picture. Earth's kingdom is an upright equilateral triangle, a pyramid, if you will. The top few are the richest, most powerful, and influential people whose main desire in life is the selfish quest for money and power. This group would also include those bureaucratic power brokers in governmental positions who levy that power and authority over us. The individuals beneath them consecutively hold less and less power and wealth, a hierarchy extending downward to the base, where dwell the multitude of the poorest and least noticed of society. Those in power at the top wield the most influence, enabling them to take control of most things, financially and socially, controlling the others in order to maintain their status. (This is *not* to say *all* wealthy people are evil; those know the Lord can be God-fearing stewards who heed the proverb, "For the *love* of money (not money itself) is the root to all kinds of evil" (1 Tim. 6:10).

The chosen methodology of the powerful, whether knowingly or unknowingly, is mind control which the Bible defines as a controlling spirit or "witchcraft". Because this group owns and controls vast media outlets, they control the messaging and narratives fed to the viewers, readers, and listeners. Through advertising and mass marketing, major corporations inculcate consumers with carnal desires. The music industry has created an art form to extol the praises of immorality, enticing its listeners to debauchery and immoral conduct. Hollywood has decayed into a cesspool of brainwashing images of immoral living and digital fantasy. Then there's the stranglehold of the public educational system, which attempts to indoctrinate young minds with foolish and evil notions like critical race theory and gender identity.

At the exclusion of teaching the true history of our great country, which was founded upon Judeo–Christian principles, American history is rewritten in order to denigrate its character while concurrently concealing the horrors of socialism. Through these informational conduits the carnal desires and ideas of fallen man filter down and are presented in such a way as to be pleasing and appealing to the senses. As these things are foisted upon the unsuspecting carnal masses, their inherent, sinful lusts take control over them in their fallen state. They buy into these empty notions, enriching not themselves, but only the so-called "elites" above them in the pecking order.

The system is further infiltrated by dishonest and greedy attorneys who manipulate the legal system and corrupt justice for notoriety and monetary gain. These spiritually dead desires, these "values," filter down the pyramid to be ingested by the unwitting souls beneath. The masses are continually bombarded with promises of good things from hitting the lottery to winning bogus lawsuits. Yet always hidden within this mindset is the downside resulting from their wanton greed and moral decay: societal collapse.

And the one behind all this wretched activity is none other than the "father of all lies," Satan himself, for he "masquerades as an angel of light" (2 Cor.11:14). He promises us the world, but he never delivers; he only escalates our lust for more. The devil always tempts you with the "product" but never reveals the price tag: drug addiction, broken families, obesity, poverty, and so forth. Once you've fallen, he'll even taunt you for having done so.

Understanding this ruse helps to explain why celebrities are idolized, yet show little evidence of contentment. Simply look at the Johnny Depp/Amber Heard court case as one current example. Both have made millions at the box office and have achieved fame and fortune in their lives. Yet their lifestyle of bickering, drug and alcohol addiction, and abusiveness was shamelessly exposed and on display for all to see—all for the sake of proving oneself "right" and winning financial gain in civil court. Have they found "peace and contentment" from the things promised in this world? Would you, in your adoration of fame and fortune, trade your ordinary, everyday lifestyle for this?

Without adherence to the guidance of a perfect God of truth, we have *all* fallen prey to the devil's lies and schemes. Deception is the main strategy in the devil's playbook. He is the puppeteer behind every person who is oblivious to the reality that they are detached from the grace of a perfect and moral God—a grace which is available to every person alive *if they so choose*. In fact, admit it, the devil's greatest deception of all is to make you believe *he doesn't exist!*

▼ . . . . Jesus at the Bottom

God's kingdom, on the other hand, is the reverse: an upside-down equilateral triangle with the poorest and humblest people on the top (the up-turned base) with an all-powerful God, Jesus at the bottom, the humble servant of all. "Whoever wants to become great among you must be your servant" (Matt.20:26, Jesus speaking). Being the most powerful, Jesus chose to humble Himself for the sake of all humanity. Divesting His divine throne in heaven, He came as a baby in humble surroundings as the incarnate "man-God," Jesus. In His prime of life, He bore the punishment for *all* the sin in the world, past, present, and future, in order that those of us who believe in Him can be restored to being the sons and daughters of the living God as was intended from the beginning. In, or may I say, *upon* Him, we place our trust and faith in the truth, for *He is Truth.* Jesus declared, "I am the way, the *truth* and the life" (John 14:6a). He came to redeem us from the kingdom of Satan, the liar who entices us with not only thoughtless power and recklessness abandon, but subtle underlying negative and degraded attitudes.

For Jesus Himself said, "Blessed are the meek, for they shall inherit the earth" (Matt.5:5). For the doubter, the cynic, the unbeliever who may at this point have become skeptical hearing this and is thinking, "I don't wish to become a pushover." Let me say yes, Jesus was meek—but *not weak*. He had command over nature, causing the raging sea to calm. He confronted and overturned the tables of the corrupt money changers in the temple. He defiantly faced the religious leaders of His day who didn't recognize Him as the Messiah. His determined mission in this world was to save unbelievers like you and me by *willingly* subjecting Himself in obedience to His Father to the agony and torture of dying in our place *out of love for us.*

Wouldn't you admit, apart from being willing to die for one of your own children whom you love, would you have the same courage and boldness to suffer and die for the ones who shouted out, "Crucify him"? Would you die for the guards who humiliated you and spat in your face, forced a crown of thorns into your scalp, flogged your back thirty-nine times until your skin and muscles were torn apart by lead-tipped cat-o'-nine tails? Would you die for the man who "washed his hands of the responsibility" of sending you to the cross? Would you die for the Roman soldiers who shamefully nailed your naked body to the cross, leaving you to die the excruciatingly painful death of crucifixion? Would you have had the courage to voluntarily die for the people hurling insults at you while you suffered? Would you say, "Forgive them for they know not what they do"? And let me ask in all candor, would you even be willing to die for *your own* child who has completely rejected *you* as a parent? No, that sort of courage comes only from a divine Source who *loves unconditionally.*

I would submit, in accordance with the selfish world system, dying for the sake of your enemy would *never* take place. It would violate the haughty, perverted values you learned that were set forth by demonic influence over you. Jesus' sacrifice, dying for us—the enemies of God—could only occur under the backdrop of an eternal realm that declares, "Love your enemies and pray for those who persecute you" (Matt.5:44). From the vantage point of God's eternity, this physical realm and everything you can acquire in it is a flash in the pan and does not compare to His inexhaustible kingdom's majesty and riches. If one could place a time scale on "forever," this life is just a blip on the screen. This world will flash past before your eyes.

For as much as our curiosity is to *define* eternity, the more important thing for us to do is *strive* for things of an eternal nature which will remain long after this trip through time and space is over. This is God's perfect will: that we, all of mankind, would find God's perfect eternal will for our lives. It is 180° contrary to the will of His adversary, the devil, whose evil intent is to foment rebellion against God and His divine purposes, using hapless, spiritually blind individuals as playthings throughout the earth. This is the key to finding true meaning and real purpose in our lives. God can clear our minds, making it possible for us to understand why evil is found in the world. If you'll allow it, God can come in to fill that empty spiritual void He placed within all of us, the void that motivates us to yearn for knowledge of the eternal. And He can fill us with His resurrection power to overcome sinfulness and to rise above evil.

At the risk of sounding redundant and trite, the written Word is our "owner's manual," a guide, a "road map" that leads us through this temporal world into ways beneficial to health and true happiness. It is authored by the Maker of humankind Himself. It cannot be effectively read primarily through the intellect, although it will challenge you on that level, but it must be read from the deeper, inner man, stripped away of his outer coating. This is because it is the Holy, living Spirit of God appealing to the stillborn, dead spirit within man. God's Word is Spirit to spirit. Read in this manner, it is the mirror through which you come to see *yourself* in the light of truth. When you read the Bible, the Bible reads you! Not only that, it is also Jesus' "autobiography," the means for God to reveal Himself to us—*identifiably* through God in *human form* so that we can identify with Him man-to-man *and* Spirit to spirit. It is solid, eternal truth.

Chapter 12

Your Place in Eternity

"Blessed are those who have not seen and yet have believed" (John 20:29b).

*W*e believe first, *then* we see. Again, this is the upside-down triangle, an oxymoron not readily understood by the carnal man. What's less understood is this: the moment we choose to believe is the moment we become citizens of eternity. Below, I will embellish upon the following Scriptures from my own point of view. "And God has raised us up with Christ and seated us with Him in the heavenly realms in Christ Jesus" (Eph.2:6). Before I follow up with my commentary, Hebrews 10:12 says, "But when this priest (Jesus) had offered *for all time* one sacrifice for sins, He sat down at the right hand of God." Now, for some background...

When a person comes to Christ, Jesus comes by invitation into that person's heart to "live and dine with him." This is the point at which one is saved from his sins, *the moment of salvation.* By Jesus entering in, our formerly "dead" carnal spirit comes alive by virtue of the Holy Spirit of Christ coming in alongside it and making it so. Spiritually, we are "resurrected to life," in a sense, *resuscitated,* and the two spirits become alive as one. From this point on, through the eyes of Father God, we are identified with His Son. We now have *become* a son or daughter of the living God, adopted into God's family. The believer is now identified with and "clothed in" Christ. A picture of this comes about through water baptism where the new believer publicly exhibits his newfound faith by being submerged underwater, symbolizing Jesus' death, burial, and descent into hell. When he re-emerges from the water, he is identifying himself as "resurrected with Christ." In the next few pages, I will allude to the judgment and those wearing white robes as being identified with Jesus as a son or daughter of God. The white robes represent cleanliness, the stain of sin removed. We are identified with, or "wearing Christ." We have now been seated under God's wing of protection from eternal, spiritual death.

Review the above Scriptures. On the one hand, Hebrews 10:12 places Jesus seated at the right hand of the Father in heaven. On the other hand, Ephesians 2:6 states we are "*seated with Him*" in the heavenly realms *in Christ Jesus*," not "*will be* seated," but "we *are* seated." The question is this: how can we remain in this physical world while at the same time be seated with Jesus in heaven? Here's my assessment. In the same way Jesus came to earth by descending "*vertically*" down from heaven to earth, intersecting with the left-to-right, *horizontal* linear timeline, we who have become believers have undergone that same intersection of time and eternity. (This imagery ironically forms *a cross!*). We are "in Christ" and now have our eternal destination secured, that is, heaven. Like God occupying time eternal, we are there now as much as we are here now. (Think upon *The Lord's Prayer,* "Your kingdom come, your will be done, on earth as it is in heaven").

"Eternal is that in which each moment exists in its full strength—immovable and unchangeable"[25]

In fact, even though my sins got forgiven the moment I received Christ, He had already died for those sins 2,000 years ago. My sins were forgiven then, but that salvation wasn't applied to me until I allowed a moment in time to intersect with that point of eternity! That infinitesimal speck of what we call "time" became eternity for me the moment I believed. At that moment, the seed of Jesus was planted in me by the

Holy Spirit the same way it was planted in the womb of the Virgin Mary. Now my spirit which has become combined with Jesus' Spirit is seated in heaven at my eternal destination, even though my flesh still occupies time and space here on earth for whatever length of time that might be. I remind you, time in eternal heaven does not exist, even though we think of eternity as being "a long time." My guess is, to coin a term, that it is simply one "forever moment." So too, was the moment of salvation when I invited Jesus into my heart that I became enjoined to him in His eternal abode.

So for me, everything in this physical world is a passing phase. My Father, the Creator in heaven who is able to continuously bring into existence provision for all our needs, will provide for all eternity. I will witness firsthand the splendor of His creative imagination. I laughed the first time I was told, "You'll never see a U-Haul being pulled by a hearse." According to the wisdom of Solomon, who had everything a man could have, said without God, all the gain of this world is meaningless, "a chasing after the wind" (Eccles.1:14). What's more, he asserted, in this world, "With much wisdom comes much sorrow; the more knowledge, the more grief." (Eccles.1:18).

Therefore, everyone, including the most brilliant people on this earth, will be forever confounded, chasing after answers to the great beyond and the great within in futility as long as they reject the notion there is one greater than themselves. The search for answers to the infinite will be, quite naturally, an endless struggle, for there is no end to its uncovering; so too will be the frustration of finding answers leading only to discover those answers never fully explain it! For all the astute thinking over the ages, has there even once been a person who died with the satisfaction of knowing it all? I think not, and there never will be. But as a believer, I *know* I will leave this world confident that I have secured for myself a portion of the very thing that baffled me throughout life; my place in eternity. "For now we see through a glass, darkly, but then face to face . . . then I shall know" (1 Cor.13:12 NKJV)

If only more souls who "think big" would instead humbly "think small" to admit they are limited by the finite. To "play god" is to reject the one who holds their breath and heartbeat in His hand. The common misconception at one time was everything in the cosmos revolved around the earth. If only more deep thinkers would humble themselves to admit the world does not revolve around their personal, puny world of what they consider to be the world of superior intelligence, but realize that their meager, carnal substance pales in comparison to that great beyond they wish to subdue. If only they'd become more aware of the fragility of their own lives, that in a few short years they'll be brought to account for their hubris. Physical death *will* eventually gather us all up. That includes those who reject the notion that God's eternal *moral* statutes are congruent with His orderly *physical* laws.

The physical world was set in place, in part, to convey the omnipotence of an all-powerful God and to lead us to an understanding of His eternal perfection. It was also intended to convey the truth of the perfection of His holiness.

> "The wrath of God is being revealed from heaven against all the godlessness and wickedness of men who suppress the truth by their wickedness, since what may be known about God is plain to them, because *God has made it plain to them.* For since the creation of the world God's invisible qualities—His eternal power and divine nature—*having clearly been seen,* being understood from what has been made, so that *men are without excuse.*" (Rom.1:18–20, *italics* mine).

Death Comes to Us All

Have you ever heard someone describe a near-death experience with the statement, "I saw my life flash before my eyes?" Perhaps you are one who has made this comment but were fortunately spared the fatal outcome. Do you wonder how this can be, your whole life flashing before you—every event, every memory—in the blink of an eye? I'd like to take a stab at this by reminding you the purpose of this book, understanding *eternity*. In my view, all of eternity exists within the tiniest fraction of time, which is *immeasurable,* at least in finite terms because, I'll say it again, time and space are uniquely fitted only to this three-dimensional space along a lateral, "left to right" time span. In that moment, all of our time on earth is reduced down to one flashing instant. What does this mean to the believer?

The previous assertion is "the gospel according to Reverend Rich," in that the instant we take our last breath is yet another example of the intersection of time and eternity spoken of earlier in this commentary. Scripturally, according to the Gospel of Jesus Christ, "We are confident, yes, well pleased rather to be *absent* from the body and to be *present* with the Lord" (2 Cor.5:8 NKJV, *italics* mine). The instant we die, we must turn and face eternity and judgment. Good news for the believer: our reward is at hand! *But,* this comes as horrific news for the unbeliever.

Second Corinthians 5 and Revelation 20 describe two thrones of judgment. Second Corinthians 5:10 describes "the judgment seat of Christ," also known as "the mercy seat," whereupon all the believers in Christ will stand before God, wearing a "white robe of salvation." This judgment is not in regard to our salvation as believers, for when we had the opportunity when were alive, we accepted Christ as Lord and His sacrifice for our sin. Because I am in Christ, I am clothed in His righteousness, in a white robe. "This righteousness from God comes through faith in Jesus Christ to *all* who believe" (Rom.3:22, *italics* mine).

Because Jesus was punished for and paid the price for our sins at Calvary, God, in His perfect wisdom and justice, cannot punish two people for the same "crime." What I'm being judged for at the mercy seat are the good works I did while in this world to advance God's kingdom. Whatever shortfall is revealed (evidenced in that instant with my life "flashing before my eyes") will result in my not receiving all the rewards God had reserved for me, yet my salvation for all eternity is secure. "For we must all appear before the judgment seat of Christ, that each one may receive what is due him for the things done while in the body" (2 Cor. 5:10). I will be rewarded for the selfless deeds I did for the sake of advancing God's kingdom. My sins do not exist because I am "in Christ" who already took my punishment. I am covered by *His* righteousness, "clothed in white." When I accepted Christ as my Savior, my name was written in the Book of Life.

However, Revelation 20:11 paints a grim picture for those outside of God's plan for salvation. Living one's life without accepting the *free gift* of forgiveness of sins that comes *free of charge* from Jesus Christ, the unsaved person will find himself not standing before the mercy seat at judgment, but before the Great White Throne of Judgment. The moment the unbeliever dies, just as the believer, he will stand before God to give an account for his or her life. Your life has passed and the period of grace that was given to you while living on earth is now past; the opportunity to receive the *free gift* of salvation no longer exists. Your life will "flash before your eyes," and you will be held to account for all the good *and bad* you've done. Sadly, your sins are *not* covered and paid for since you did not accept by faith the *free gift* of salvation that was offered to you while you were alive. You see, a gift can be offered to you, but only be *received* by taking it and opening it. But *you rejected the free gift!* (Notice all the emphases I've placed upon *free gift*). Spoiler alert: you cannot enter into an infinite, holy, perfect place where there is no sin, wearing a mortal, decaying "*sin-stained outer garment.*" You need to be "clothed" by Jesus' perfection, wearing *His* "white robe." To enter into a place of perfection, where sin is nonexistent, you must become perfect. Only God's perfection will do. If you have chosen to believe in Jesus, you are in Christ, who is God, and you have been *made* perfect.

But now, as your life is on display flashing before you and your Maker, you will find yourself desperately trying to explain why you thought it was foolishness to accept the free gift of salvation. Because you are uncovered and exposed, you will try to explain your way out of every situation where you faltered, every lie, every misdeed, every act of malice, every word from your mouth that was ever spoken. You will attempt to claim your good deeds outweighed your bad, but to no avail. Romans 3:23 asserts, "*All* have sinned and fall short of the glory of God."

Like Adam and Eve desperately trying to sew together fig leaves to cover their nakedness, you will be hopelessly exposed, standing naked before God. Only God could cover Adam and Eve's sin by shedding the blood of an animal to give them skins to wear as a covering. Only God's covering will do because your own works are thoroughly insufficient in comparison to perfection to cover your own sin! Only the shed blood of Jesus Christ will do.

In your lifetime here on earth you had, perhaps numerous times, been offered that covering in simplistic terms, but you refused. If only you had accepted the free gift of forgiveness through Jesus and His covering of His shed blood, you would not have found yourself in this desperately frightening predicament because according to God's perfect laws, all who have sinned are deserving of death. "The wages of sin is death, but the *gift of God is eternal life in Christ Jesus* our Lord" (Rom.6:23, *italics* mine). God had provided Jesus for you as a way out to avoid all this, but because you thought it foolish, you were too proud to accept it.

Now, your final destination is the lake of fire. All this could have been avoided had you had simply humbled yourself when you had the chance with child-like faith to believe God's report, His *simple* plan of salvation. You see, hell was originally created for Satan and his demons who rebelled against God in heaven. But because humankind, deceived by the devil and his minions, has joined the rebellion against God, hell had to be enlarged to accompany the additional rebels. "Therefore, Sheol [hell] has enlarged itself and opened its mouth beyond measure; their glory and their multitude and their pomp, and he who is jubilant, shall descend into it. People will be brought down; each man shall be humbled, and the eyes of the lofty shall be humbled." (Isa.5:14–15, NKJV). God never intended His creation to die in hell. God is a gentleman.

He doesn't force Himself upon us. He gave everyone *free will* to love Him, but in their deception, mankind freely chose to remain in sin and rebellion over choosing to believe He sent His Son to die in our place.

Revelation 20:11–15 says:

> "Then I saw a great white throne and Him who was seated on it. Earth and sky fled from His presence, and there was no place for them. And I saw the dead, great and small, standing before the throne, and books were opened. Another book was opened which is the book of life. The dead were judged according to what they had done . . . each person was judged according to what he had done . . . if anyone's name was not found written in the book of life, he was thrown into the lake of fire."

Notice, there were "books" (plural) and "another book," (singular). The "other" book is the Book of Life. Once you've invited Jesus into your heart, you are *saved* and your name becomes registered in it. Your name is sealed in the Book of Life. The believer has "books" also, recounting the deeds done in the flesh, the evidence to condemn them. But in God's court, there is *true* justice. Because Jesus became sin for me, and was found guilty by His Father and took the punishment for sin on the cross that I deserved, that evidence is thrown out. It is like "double jeopardy." No person can be charged again for a crime for which he has been found not-guilty, nor can two people be punished for the same crime. Those *books,* that "evidence" against the believer, is inadmissible. Jesus, my "advocate" paid my "fine," my penalty. The only book left to judge me is the Book of Life, where my name will be found, and I am *acquitted* and sent to be in heaven for all eternity.

Unsaved people are not recorded in the Book of Life. Their fate has been sealed. The preponderance of evidence against them is recorded in "the books." They will be held to account for their sins, the penalty for which is death. They had no advocate to defend them, and no one to pay the debt for they rejected Jesus, the free gift of salvation, the payment for their sins. Their anger against God will be fierce, but it was that same animosity and rejection toward their heavenly Father that prevented them from accepting the simple truth of God's Word while alive on the earth. They preferred to believe "the lie" of Satan, the enemy of God, who rebelled against Him. The devil had succeeded in blinding the eyes of the unbeliever to haplessly trick him into likewise rebelling against God and His Word. This is the only playbook the devil has, to deceive the minds of men, causing them to become condemned to eternal death. And how ironic the way the devil deceives people into thinking *he* does not exist! What better way to get back at the Father of all creation, whom he hates, than to take out one of His offspring! To borrow a phrase, without belief in Jesus, "the world is going to hell in a hand basket."

Resurrected to Eternal Life and Death

Jesus was resurrected from the dead. There can be no doubt. No person could have survived such torture, scourging, and crucifixion, followed by being pierced with a sword through His chest. He was literally beaten and torn beyond recognition. Yet, the Bible account references over 500 witnesses to his resurrected, living body (1 Cor.15:6). Scholars, lawyers, and physicians, many of whom were atheists and agnostics endeavoring to disprove the resurrection, cannot provide a logical reason how this happened. Some, by way of investigating, became believers themselves (for example: Lee Strobel's, *The Case for Christ*).[26]

Acceptance of the narrative set forth by the Sanhedrin, (which was the ruling Jewish priests and scribes at that time) that His disciples had stolen Jesus' body should be considered an outright farce. Apart from a regiment of Roman soldiers posted at the tomb, which was sealed with a huge rock, all of the disciples, *out of fear,* went into hiding when Jesus was crucified, thinking they might be next. Also, how do you account for the boldness they all received upon seeing Him alive, and how later, at Pentecost, being filled with the Holy Spirit, how they dedicated their lives testifying to those events…even unto *death*? All but one of the original apostles eventually were martyred for their testimonies. Would *you* face death to promote a hoax?

"But Christ has indeed been raised from the dead, the first fruits of those who have fallen asleep" (1 Cor.15:20). *All* will be raised from the dead to face judgment. Again, here's the truly bad news for unbelievers because Jesus himself said, "for a time is coming when all who are in their graves will hear His voice and come out—those who have done good will rise to life, and those who have done evil will rise to be condemned" (John 5:28). "They will weed out of His kingdom everything that causes sin and all who do evil. They will throw them into the blazing furnace, where there will be weeping and gnashing of teeth" (Matt.13:41b–42, Jesus speaking).

Have you ever stopped to consider how a soul thrown into hell can be, for all eternity, "weeping" and "gnashing" his teeth? It is at this point, based on the above quote from Jesus, I will assert this position: that *all* men, saved and unsaved, will be resurrected to an incorruptible body. Although Scripture does not directly state this, it clearly infers it. For how else can a soul, a *person* if you will, be forever tortured in a lake of fire? A corruptible body would instantly be consumed by such an event. Even standing at the throne before the Lord at judgment, a "consuming fire" would annihilate any mortal body. "You cannot see my face, for no one may see me and live" (Exod.33:20).

Therefore, the same immortal, incorruptible body given to the believer at the resurrection will be the same immortal, incorruptible body given the unbeliever. The only difference is what his "seed" has yielded (sin unto death or righteousness unto life) and what will become his final destination. "Then they will go away to eternal punishment, but the righteous to eternal life" (Matt. 25:46, again, Jesus speaking). "Whether people want it or not, believe it or not, the resurrection of every person who has ever lived will happen, and an eternal existence in one of two places will be a reality."[27] "I am going to open your graves and bring you up from them" (Ezek.37:12).

Take to heart what I'm saying. We believers in Christ, who will enjoy being in the presence of God wearing an eternal body suit, eating from the Tree of Life, drinking living water, feeling the coolness of the day walking beside Jesus, and having every hunger and desire of our hearts satisfied at the Lord's table, *for all eternity,* should be mindful of the lost multitudes of unbelievers surrounding us today who will be forever cursing God, tortured, thirsting, suffering, hungering, and crying out for relief alone in *their* eternal body suits. It's saddening to me to think that refusing something as simple as humbly taking a child-like leap of faith to believe God's Word would result in an eternity of regret for not seeing it. We only get one chance in this lifetime *under God's grace.* It only takes a moment in time to invite Jesus into our hearts, a moment where time can intersect with eternity, and instantly become saved from condemnation. "The Lord protects the simple-hearted; when I was in great need, He saved me" (Ps.116:6).

Apart from the never-ending torment of isolation in fire and being forever devoured by worms, this rumination may be the worst of all tortures: "If only I had had simple faith to accept His mercy and believed in Him, I could have been spared from all this! My sin would *not* have caused me to be here!"—in an unending, torturous, "forever moment of time." Remember this, God doesn't *send* people to hell. Your rejection of God's simple plan for salvation seals your fate. By not believing in Jesus whom the Father sent to reach out to you, *you send yourself to hell.* You see, "good people" don't go to heaven and "bad people" don't go to hell. *Saved* people go to heaven; *unsaved* people go to hell! Simply put, just "believe and see."

The fires of hell and the curses that will befall you outside of God's will are not the result of Him cursing you. It is because of your wrong choices. It is the same when a parent warns a child not to run out in the street into traffic. It isn't the parent driving the car that might run over the child. It is the result of the child's wrong choice to not obey their father and look both ways as instructed. The same holds true when we neglect Father God's instruction. We subject ourselves to the consequences of our own rebellious actions. God points out curses only as a consequence to our sinful nature. He *wants* you protected! It is why He sent His Son—to provide a way out of our hopeless condition!

I implore you to believe this. Your curiosity led you to read this in an effort to solve the age-old question, "What is eternity?" The answer is quite clear and surprisingly simple. *God is eternity* because He is eternal. He lives outside time and space. He is the same yesterday, today, and forever. He set forth all of what you see as proof of His majesty. He is Love. He provided a bridge for you to cross into His realm in the form of the sinless man, Jesus, fully human just like you, yet fully God. He appointed a moment in "history" to coincide with "His story" of eternity. Out of a heart of compassion for all humanity, He sent His Son Jesus to become rejected by Him and voluntarily bear the punishment for our sinfulness. And because He is Love, He permits His loved ones the *freedom* to choose to love Him or reject Him. Otherwise, it would not be true love but coercion. He won't force Himself upon anyone, but His invitation is open to every single person on the planet. His wish is for all to be saved and become His adopted sons and daughters. As it is with how you love your children and want them to be part of your life, so it is with Father God, but on a much grander scale. He wants us to be a part of His life, not only on special occasions like birthdays and Christmas, but from everlasting to everlasting—for all eternity!

God gave us five senses to bear witness to his creation. God also set into nature invisible things like ultraviolet and infrared light, radio waves, colorless gases, and things microscopic to convey the reality of an unseen, invisible spirit world where angels and demons exist. He set eternity in every man's heart and the intelligence enough to connect this yearning to the witness of an ever-expanding universe as a clue to His eternal nature. He embedded within us a curiosity to explore the mysteries of nature, in order to draw out the detective in every one of us to piece together clues to solve the mystery and reveal the author behind it all.

Jesus said: "*I* am the *way,* the *truth* and the *life.* No one comes to the Father except through me" (John 14:6, *italics* mine). Don't allow the devil, the "father of lies," to cloud your thinking about this. This is for real. This is literally a matter of life and death, heaven or hell. You've been given the freedom of choice. You get to decide for yourself whether the conclusion of this book about eternity ends on a happy note or whether it ends as a tragedy. *You get to decide* where you'll spend eternity. *It's up to you* whether the definition of eternity ultimately translates to eternal pain or eternal pleasure. You are free to continue being deceived into believing the lies or be free to believe the truth; free to willfully hold on to foolish pride or be free to humbly accept mercy; free to remain spiritually dead or be free to live eternally. You are by nature born spiritually *dead* in your sins. *His* Spirit is *life everlasting. Your* spirit is *death everlasting.* He's God; you're not. He's the potter; you're the clay. He's the boss; He sets the rules. As in any sporting event when you break the rules, you're tossed. But this is not about an innocuous game to be toyed with; this is as serious as a heart attack. This is for the sake of your everlasting life and must be treated with the gravest sense of sobriety.

"In this way love is made complete among us so that we will have confidence on the day of judgment, because in this world we are like Him" (1 John 4:17 *italics,* mine)

Yet, because He is Love, God's mercies are renewed continually giving you broad opportunities to see things His way, through His eyes, the eyes of eternity. In Jesus, you are clothed in Christ's righteousness under the wing of God's protection. Outside of His plan of salvation, outside of that protection, you stand subjected to the curses, the pitfalls, and damage wrought by sin. You stand vulnerable, naked, and alone without *covering,* completely separated from God and His goodness toward you. The offer remains for as long as you live, but your days to accept the plan are numbered. Tomorrow is not guaranteed to anyone. "I tell you, now is the time of God's favor, now is the day of salvation" (2 Cor.6:2b). You have just so many of those "now" moments while you live restricted by time. But all you need is one tiny microsecond, one unimaginably small "yoctosecond" to secure your eternal salvation.

"I have set before you life and death, blessings and curses. *Now choose life,* so that you and your children may live . . . For the Lord *is* your life" (Deut.30:19b–20a, *italics* mine).

Chapter 13

Epilogue

It Is Entirely All about Eternity

As any responsible parent would know, it is incumbent upon them to provide a secure home for their children. They would provide a roof overhead, a place to rest the child's head, provisions enough to feed, clothe, and nurture their offspring. There would be an abundance of love and caring available to the helpless infant. There would be late nights of comforting a colicky babe. There would be moments of despair as well as moments of great pleasure. Over time, the parent would see evidence of growth, a time to enable the child to rise and walk. At first you hold them by the hands and slowly begin to let them go and walk upright on their own. You train and mold the child to grasp his God-given talents and abilities. You help them to develop and hone those skills. You employ discipline to keep them from harming themselves. You teach them responsibility by issuing to them duties like washing the dishes, making their bed, taking out the trash.

As they age, the stakes rise and there comes friction and rebellion as they pass through the emotionally painful stages of puberty. The former child, now a young adult, becomes more obstinate, thinking he knows better than you. But eventually there will come a time to break the ties and a time when you know to when let go and promote them to independence. Even once the child has become an adult, the love and caring never ceases. You always long for their presence after they've flown the coop.

If you, the reader, have experienced any phase of this with your own children, you sometimes wonder how this son or daughter, once a wee little embryo from the womb, has become fully grown in what seems to have been a very short span of time. Reflecting on all this, we realize the importance of our role as parents. We hope as the child matures, he comes to this realization as well and attaches an importance to their link in the generational chain.

Take It All The Way Back

Nowadays, there seems to be an obsession to trace one's ancestry. We hunger for knowledge of our past, hoping we'll uncover some dramatic secret concealed in our lineage. Many hope to find some important person who attained wealth and notoriety. Some hope to find royalty. However, no one wishes to be descended from the town drunk or anyone else of scandalous repute! Eventually the paper trail runs out, and the DNA has spoken to the percentages of mixed nationalities connected to your makeup. Maybe that was all you desired to know, but still you've arrived at a historical dead end.

Interestingly, the seeker seldom realizes there is much more to the story. Our ancestral linkage traces back well beyond that of recorded history. Intellectually, there remain unknowns, for the natural man can only glean from that which has been passed along in written form. Yet there remains another source of written history for us to consider that most people ignore.

The Written Word of God!

I challenge you to step outside your carnal, intellectual way of thinking for just one moment. As a matter of necessity, I ask of you to please drop all your preconceived, so-called "logical" notions of how you think you know better. Open up your mind.

Now pretend you're at the movies. In the darkness of the theater, you allow yourself to enter into the mind of the director. You allow yourself to believe there really is a universe far, far away where the forces of good and evil battle. You allow yourself to believe there really is a Matrix; that folks are suspended in a dream world, and Neo and Morpheus truly exist. You allow yourself to escape into an unknown world for the sake of diversion and entertainment.

I've deliberately drawn you into the realm of movie fantasy because it is with *certainty* that I believe the spiritual blindness in our world has been aided and abetted by a scheme to distract the natural man from the reality of a true, unseen world behind everything that can be seen. It is fantastical, but *it is not fantasy!* Were it not for a *real* unseen world, there would never have been lodged in the minds of writers and movie makers to counterfeit the notion. It is within this mindset I wish you to enter into the mind of this believer and consider the following scenario. And just for the sake of argument, I *beg* you to open your spiritual ears to hear and spiritual eyes to see.

It is written, God created the heavens and the earth—providing a secure home for His creation: *His children.* He was our original Father, our parent, and out of love He wanted a family in His own likeness. He breathed life into our lungs and enabled His living Spirit to dwell within us connecting us, not unlike an umbilical cord, to Himself. He had beforehand provided a home for His offspring, vegetation for food, water for drink, an atmosphere containing oxygen so we can continue to breathe, He provided *the balance of nature.* He created every living thing to have seed to replicate itself "after its own kind" to sustain the established order of things in nature. As a loving Father, He walked with us in the cool of the day to teach us how to "walk upright." He gave us duties and responsibilities, giving us charge over His creation. In the same way as our parents taught us not to touch the hot stove for our own good, He issued one edict, "You must not eat from the Tree of the Knowledge of Good and Evil, for when you eat of it you will surely die" (Gen.2:17b).

Yet, in foolishness, we rebelled like the average teenager. In ignorance, we thought we knew better; we thought we could "be like God"— even though we *already were!* In disobedience, we alone were at fault for "burning our fingers atop the stove" as warned, creating a disconnect of our living spirit to God's living Spirit, causing our "spiritual lifeline" to be severed. We instantly "*surely died,*" spiritually speaking. The decaying process of aging thus began, which would eventually lead to our certain *physical death.* It also brought death to the perfect relationship with our Father, for in shame of our nakedness, *relationally* we could no longer "walk upright" with our Father again.

While He did not tolerate our offense, He Himself shed the blood of an innocent animal to lovingly clothe us in an animal skin to cover our wrong, our nakedness, our exposure to sin. Yet, as any parent would, He continued to love His children. God further knew He had to allow His child to continue in his own willfulness because the perfect, selfless love He had for us could never be returned to Him by force. He had to let go in the hope his child's heart would someday return to Him freely.

As would the natural parent, He disciplined us in love by banishing us from the home He had provided because in His garden there grew another tree, "The Tree of Life" (that is, *Eternal Life*). Had we eaten from the Tree of Life while in that sinful condition, we would have remained immortally rebellious and *eternally* in our sin with no hope for redemption, only a future of suffering and destruction. You see, instead of the seed of immortality God had planted when He breathed into us, spawning *eternal life and connection to Himself,* the seed of sin was now sown, causing death to enter into what otherwise would have been an eternity with God walking beside us. The seed of sin replicates itself into death and spiritual disconnection. What might have been interpreted as an act of anger toward us was instead, an act of mercy, an unselfish letting go of the one He loves. And because of His perfect love for us, we must consider this:

Unselfish Love in the Flesh

Given the fact our God lives in eternity, not bogged down with time and space, knowing the beginning from the end, it stands to reason He knew the events of how His creation would unfold, our rebellion and failure to obey Him. Just as with the natural parent, knowing their child's mischievous tendencies, would have to keep a watchful eye on his children to heed the warning, saying, "Don't run into the street," He knew we would become disconnected from the eternal life that He granted us from the beginning. He knew we would fall away disconnected from the "family tie." He knew His creation of mankind, through sin, would careen out of control in every vile and ugly manner and in essence, "leave home" stubbornly, not wishing to look back. He had to know in order to restore us to sonship, there would have to be a plan set in place to secure His children's redemption. He became:

"the Lamb who was slain from the creation of the world" (Rev.13:8b).

I can only imagine the conversation within the Godhead when the concept of creating a family was considered. The three persons of the Godhead—Father, Son, and Holy Spirit—in joint counsel, had to have concluded the mission was doomed to failure from the start, given the fact His children would be given the right of free will..In consideration of an infinite combination of scenarios, they knew blood would have to be shed to clothe their naked children when sin would be exposed in them. They had to have concluded, "Without the shedding of blood there could be no forgiveness" (Heb.9:22).

They purposed and fashioned a structure of rituals for the Israelites involving animal sacrifice to mimic what God had done in the garden to cover their sins and to suggest what was to come. The animals would be required to be "spotless" specimens; otherwise, they would be rejected like sinful Adam had to be ousted from the garden. Because His original creation, Adam, could not be perfect in obedience to His authority, they had to have thought a perfect human being would need to become a substitute for Adam. They needed a "second Adam." And that second Adam had to become the perfect, spotless, sinless blood sacrifice for the sins of mankind; all of this a picture to draw man's attention to their Savior.

I can now imagine the Son stepping forward, saying to the Father, "I'll do it. I will humble myself by stepping down from my glory in heaven and become a vulnerable human baby, grow up, be obedient to my father on earth and my Father in heaven and never sin. For the sake of our children and their everlasting salvation, I will voluntarily suffer and shed *my* blood by becoming the perfect blood sacrifice for sin. I will show them how much I love them by taking the punishment they deserve."

Because the sin of mankind had been passed down through the generations, sown by the sinful "seed" of Adam, a human father was out of the question. The seed had to be breathed once again in a way similar to how God breathed the breath of life into Adam—by Father God Himself. The seed of God.

"The virgin will conceive and give birth to a son" (Isa.7:14; Matt.1:23).

Father God Himself, through the person of the Holy Spirit, sowed the seed of heavenly perfection into the womb of the Virgin Mary. Therefore, Jesus was born fully God and fully man. He grew up as any child at that time, apprenticing with His adoptive father, Joseph as a carpenter. When the appointed time arrived, Jesus entered into His ministry of reconciliation, listening and obeying the voice of His Father in heaven whom He clearly heard in prayer. There was no sin in Him that could separate Him from the Father in heaven. He preached the good news of salvation speaking in parables. He dwelt among us. He sympathized with us. He brought healing to us. He fulfilled all the Old Testament prophecies attesting to His authenticity as God in the flesh. He succeeded in walking in perfection before God where Adam had failed.

I prefaced all this by imploring you to keep an open mind about these things. Most importantly, I begged you to open your spiritual eyes and ears so you can understand. So here is the kicker: Among all the miracles Jesus performed as signs and wonders to lead you to believe in Him, the only ones He performed not recorded by any other prophets in the Old Testament, was opening the eyes of the blind, the ears of the deaf, and healing the lame so they could walk.

Several times in the OT, folks were raised from the dead. A few times, loaves of bread or oil were miraculously multiplied, all of which Jesus also did with the raising of Lazarus and others, the turning of water into wine, and the feeding of the five thousand from five loaves and two fishes. Yet, does it not make you wonder why these other three miraculous signs were performed only by Jesus?

"I once was blind, but now I see."

In the whole of physical creation, we see displayed God's infinite fingerprint as a guide and a sign to lead us to the knowledge of Him. He reveals His immense majesty in how He puts on display the infinite vastness of space. He shows us how much He yearns to be close in an intimate way in how things are knitted together in all things small. He wants us to realize His commitment to loving us by focusing attention on how time "stands still" in His presence, yet it is forever and always.

I submit to you now, the three miracles cited above that only Jesus performed are also signs for you to notice! If you've kept an open mind, well terrific! Because God's call goes out to all who would "have ears to hear and eyes to see." However, this is not an end unto itself; this is a matter of the heart. One can plunge themselves into the depths of God's Word and memorize every Scripture, every chapter and verse and still remain spiritually dead in their sin. It was only when you allow the seed of His Word to be sown into your heart of hearts, *where your dead spirit dwells,* where the seed of His Eternal Spirit can spring to life and have its effect on you.

For me, it was only when I humbled myself and *earnestly* invited Him into my life, consciously using my *free will* to reconnect Him to the source of my inner being, "my spirit man," that the spiritual scales fell from my eyes. I could now *see* the Light of the Gospel. My ears could now *hear* God's Word, I could now begin to *walk* with God. My place in eternity was now settled. I now perceive God's hand at work in my life in all the circumstances and coincidences surrounding me. The mysteries of science and what it uncovers pertaining to the awesome work of the Master gives me more reason to believe in His eternal, perfect nature. He has mirrored His almighty perfection in the orderliness of all physical things.

Before coming to belief in Christ, I was but a mere pawn, a tool of the devil. It was like being one of the hapless victims in the Matrix who were lulled into a dreamland of unreality in need of rescue. I was living a lie, fighting on the side of Darth Vader against the forces of good while, through my human pride, duped into thinking I was doing all the right things. The "right thing" according to the wisdom of this world has fomented chaos, conflict, and disorder throughout the history of fallen mankind. The wisdom of God, which renders man's wisdom to foolishness, is *infinitely* higher than that of man's attempts at world peace, and is the only thing which brings the "peace that surpasses all understanding" (Phil.4:6).

Notice too, how the natural man can only mimic God's salvation plan. Isn't it interesting how many successful Hollywood storylines have a hidden Jesus figure who is willing to place his own life at risk to save others? The selflessness of the hero always tugs at the heartstrings. Then there is the supernatural. It is depicted as wondrous, exhilarating, and sometimes frightening. But this too is a cheap counterfeit designed to distract you away from the invisible, yet existent supernatural spirit realm. That is the reason I've drawn this parallel between man's phony portrayal of the unseen things to what is in reality God's heavenly kingdom versus Satan's earthly domain.

"I once was lost, but now am found."

Having the living Spirit of truth dwelling within me makes it painfully obvious how we are all in such desperate need of a Savior to rescue ourselves from ourselves and from the inherent blindness we incur from every powerful influence introduced to us in the physical realm. Without a heavenly Father to guide us, we are lost in this world without clear moral leadership. We are chained to the sinful nature. Similarly, without a mortal father in the picture, many men are statistically doomed to a life of imprisonment, corrupted and wandering, lost without a moral compass.

I can see in the light of reality how things in the finite reflect the things of God in the infinite. I can see when we make things right with our heavenly Father, the patterns in our physical existence follow suit. Short of perfection (since we remain in the finite, fallen physical realm until we pass) things just tend to make more sense. The void inside that begs the question, "What is eternity" becomes filled with the promises of the eternal God Himself! From there He can whisper to us on the inside revealing some of the mysteries that puzzle us and guide us into all wisdom. He is in there, remodeling me from the inside out, so that in Him "we can move and have our being" (Acts 17:28). The only requirement for me to enter into this relationship with Him is a broken and contrite heart and a willingness to humble myself as a child before Him who is infinitely higher than me. I must recognize my fallen state of being, my sinfulness, and trust with child-like faith that Jesus has died *in my place* for the penalty of my sinfulness through His blood sacrifice. I must believe in my heart that God raised Jesus from the dead and that He sits now at the right hand of the Father. I must also believe that I have been raised up with Him and I am "seated (us) with Him in the heavenly realms in Christ Jesus" (Eph.2:6). This means I am living in eternity right now while I am concurrently living under the stranglehold of time and space! I have been made alive in Christ; I am a new creation in Christ. I have access to my eternal Father through Christ. I am dead to sin. "I have been crucified with Christ and I no longer live, but Christ lives in me" (Gal.2:20). Right in this moment is found the *intersection of time and eternity.*

This is a matter of life or death.

Pray this prayer with me right now because "now is the time for God's favor, *now is the day of salvation*" (2 Cor.6:2b):

> Lord, I admit I have been deluded by blindness to your existence, that I have rejected you as the source of all life. Jesus, I humble myself with childlike faith to accept your sacrifice for my sin by the shedding of your blood and dying on a cross in my place. I believe you are the Christ, my Savior, and I welcome you to come into my heart right now. I believe Father God raised you from the dead in order for me to be raised with you and restored to everlasting life as His son/daughter, as an adopted child grafted into your family. Lord, I thank you for your unbounded, everlasting love, mercy and forgiveness. In the precious name of Jesus, Amen.

If you prayed that prayer *with sincerity of heart,* congratulations! Welcome to the family of the living God! In the blink of an eye, you've just allowed the infinite to intersect with the finite! You have been eternally saved from the pits of hell. You have been restored to life, *eternal life!* Your name is written in the Book of Life. Passage to your eternal destination in heaven is booked. God has answered you. Now, just wait and see how your blindness will fade and all things become new. In the words of John Eldredge, "Unplug from the clamor (the constant noise in your life), and make room for eternity in your life." (Eldredge, August 2).

Because you've *first* believed, you will now see. You asked in the finite and your answer has come from the infinite one, God. God Himself has answered you, "*Yes and Amen!*" —***Eternity Answered!***

Endnotes

1   Chambers, Oswald.. *My Utmost For His Highest.* ©1992 by Oswald
    Chambers Publications Association, Ltd. ISBN 978-1-62707-
    881-8 June 19

2   Unless otherwise indicated, Scripture references are taken from
    the HOLY BIBLE, NEW INTERNATIONAL VERSION ®. NIV ®
    Copyright © 1973,1978,1984 by the International Bible Society.
    Used by permission of Zondervan Publishing House. All rights
    reserved.

3   Sir Isaac Newton, thejohn10:10project.com

4   https://www.thefreedictionary.com/higgs+boson

5   Murray, Andrew *The Holiest of All: A Commentary of the Book
    of Hebrews*, © 1996, 2004 by Whitaker House, 1030 Hunt Valley
    Circle, New Kensington, PA 15068

6   The Slow Death of Spontaneous Generation, https://blblack.sci-
    ences.ncsu.edu/bio183de/Black/cellintro/cellintro_reading/
    Spontaneous_Generation.html

7   https://www.britannica.com/biography/
    Antonie-van-Leeuwenhoek

8   https://byjus.com/biology/unicellular-organisms/

9   Ramm, Bernard *"The Christian View of Science and Scripture"*
    ©1954 Wm. B. Eerdmans Publishing Co. p.149

10 Ibid, Ramm, p.149

[11] Ibid, Ramm, pp. 145-146

[12] Cahn, Jonathan *The Book of Mysteries.* ©2016 by Jonathan Cahn, ISBN 978-1-62998-941-9, Day 89

[13] https://www.goodreads.com/author/quotes/6521868. Edwin_Conklin

[14] Anderson, Neil T. *Daily in Christ.* ©1993 by Harvest House Publishers, Inc, Eugene, OR

[15] Stoner, P.W. Neuman, R.C. *Science Speaks.* ©1976 by Moody Press, Chicago, Il

[16] https://genius.com/ Crosby-stills-nash-and-young-teach-your-children-lyrics

[17] Tozer, A.W. *The Radical Cross: Living the Passion of Christ.* ©2005, 2009 by Zur Ltd. 978-1-60066-282-9

[18] Chambers, Oswald. *My Utmost For His Highest.* ©1992 by Oswald Chambers Publications Association, Ltd. ISBN 978-1-62707-881-8 June 23rd

[19] Gore Jr., Albert Arnold *An Inconvenient Truth* ©2006 Rodale, Inc., ISBN 1-59486-567-1

[20] https://www.politifact.com/fact-checks/2011/nov/15/americans-prosperity/ solyndra-ad-president-barack-obama-taxpayer-money/

[21] https://bethelcornerstone.org/ oswald-chambers-was-baptized-in-the-holy-spirit/

[22] https://genius.com/John-lennon-imagine-lyrics

[23] https://genius.com/ Crosby-stills-nash-and-young-teach-your-children-lyrics

[24] https://genius.com/The-animals-its-my-life-lyrics25

Murray, Andrew. *The Holiest of All: A Commentary on the Book of Hebrews.* ©1996, 2006 by Whitaker House, 1030 Hunt Valley Circle, Kensington, PA 15068

[26] Strobel, Lee. *The Case For Christ.* ©1998 Zondervan Publishing House

[27] Wommack, Andrew. *Life For Today, I & II Corinthians Edition.* ©Andrew Wommack Ministries, Inc. p.959